CAMBRIDGE
UNIVERSITY PRESS

CAMBRIDGE ENGLISH
Language Assessment
Part of the University of Cambridge

CAMBRIDGE
OFFICIAL
PREPARATION MATERIAL

Cambridge English

Compact
Advanced

Workbook with answers

T0349672

Simon Haines

Cambridge University Press
www.cambridge.org/elt

Cambridge Assessment English
www.cambridgeenglish.org

Information on this title: www.cambridge.org/9781107417908
© Cambridge University Press and UCLES 2014

This publication is in copyright. Subject to statutory exception
and to the provisions of relevant collective licensing agreements,
no reproduction of any part may take place without the written
permission of the publishers.

First published 2014

Printed in Great Britain by CPI Group (UK) Ltd, Croydon CR0 4YY

A catalogue record for this publication is available from the British Library

ISBN 978-1-107-41790-8 Workbook with answers with Audio
ISBN 978-1-107-41782-3 Workbook without answers with Audio
ISBN 978-1-107-41838-7 Teacher's Book
ISBN 978-1-107-41802-8 Student's Book with answers with CD-ROM
ISBN 978-1-107-41808-0 Student's Book without answers with CD-ROM
ISBN 978-1-107-41828-8 Class Audio CDs (2)
ISBN 978-1-107-41819-6 Student's Book Pack (Student's Book with answers with CD-ROM and Class Audios (2))
ISBN 978-1-107-41831-8 Presentation Plus DVD-ROM
ISBN 978-1-107-41832-5 Interactive ebook: Student's Book with answers
ISBN 978-1-107-41794-6 Interactive ebook: Workbook with answers

Additional resources for this publication at www.cambridge.org/compactadvanced

The publishers have no responsibility for the persistence or accuracy of URLs
for external or third-party internet websites referred to in this publication, and
do not guarantee that any content on such websites is, or will remain, accurate or
appropriate. Information regarding prices, travel timetables, and other factual
information given in this work is correct at the time of first printing but the
publishers do not guarantee the accuracy of such information thereafter.

Produced by Wild Apple

CONTENTS

1 Breaking news

Reading and Use of English

Part 7

Look at the exam task and answer these questions.

1 What do you understand by the term *citizen journalism*?
2 How is a *citizen journalist* different from a newspaper journalist?
3 When have citizen journalists provided important news stories?

Exam task

You are going to read an extract from an article. Six paragraphs have been removed from the extract.
Choose from the paragraphs A–G the one which fits each gap (1–6). There is one extra paragraph which you do not need to use.

THE RISE OF 'CITIZEN JOURNALISM'

Journalists lecture the rest of the world about the importance of change in everything from foreign policy to food labelling. Yet the same journalists dislike change as much as anyone else; their extensive experience of recommending change does not help them to accept it themselves. The fact is that journalists react to digital technology's disruption of their industry with the same anger as any groups of professionals required to rethink what they do.

1 [   ]

'Journalism' came into existence when reliable information was scarce. As newspaper publishing and distribution grew, editors had to satisfy demands for accuracy, as well as entertainment. The effort to be trusted came to be the distinguishing mark of journalism. But printing technology made journalism powerful: a few people gathered, sorted and distributed news and hoped that many people would buy it.

2 [   ]

Anyone can now publish their thoughts and their books for free to a global audience. Old fashioned print publishing by the few to the many sits uneasily next to successful 'peer-to-peer' networks.

3 [   ]

Citizens, helped by democratic technology, can at last bypass and expose these tricks but 'citizen journalism' can also simply mean a wider range of sources. Big events that leave media organisations rushing to get to the right spots are now covered by volunteer witnesses who send instant photos and videos from their mobile phones. Where established reporters fear to go – war zones being the obvious example – the voice of the ordinary citizen journalist may be the only believable news source.

4 [   ]

The attempt to get at the truth may fail or may fail to be credible. It may involve opinion and analysis as well as reportage so that the truth is understood in depth and significance. It will involve judgements under pressure about truth and public interest. We call this inexact science 'editing'. Anyone looking at the history of journalism will also notice that the organisations that do it are regularly turned upside down. Two forces do this: first, frustrated journalists who find the habits and the conventions of journalism block all attempts to get at the truth.

5 [   ]

Journalists still gather the basic news, but must also meet the need to give it meaning and context. We analyse news in the context of instant global conversations that can involve a handful of people or millions. Believers in citizen journalism argue that enforced 'democratisation' of media reduces the need for, and therefore the power of the conventional media. The forces of change may bring down media empires that fail to adapt, but they do not destroy the idea of journalism.

6 [   ]

Also the way people sample and use news and opinion is changing: they dip in and out of news all day. But the business of getting accurate basic data to consumers, of building platforms that people trust remains valuable work despite the changing background. Some 'citizen journalists' make a real contribution to this; some don't. It depends who they are. In other words, we're back where we started: making judgements about accuracy and honesty. The most important question consumers of news and opinion will ask themselves is the question they have always asked: do I trust this source to tell me something true and useful?

A Against this background, 'citizen journalism' means different things to different citizens. As a movement in media politics, citizen journalists would like to replace 'conventional media', arguing that the claims made by journalists for the trustworthiness of their work are a trick, hiding agendas which may belong to big business or government.

B Bloggers have increased the transparency of the established media by exposing errors, and acting as gossip platforms for opinion that would otherwise not circulate so far so fast. These are not all citizens, in the sense of being outside media organisations; many are journalists and many of their sources are journalists.

C However, three changes turned this shortage of public information into today's glut: the invention of radio and television, digital technology such as email, and finally the Internet. Digital communications not only increased the amount of easily-reached information but weakened the power of traditional publishing.

D I may not be in a majority in my line of work, but I like the current technology-driven chaos precisely because journalists have to go back to first principles. Let's look at the history.

E The need to know the accuracy of what you are reading or watching does not disappear because you have a lot of new ways of finding facts and other points of view. The nature of the news and opinion people now consume is changing: more varied, less formal, often like an everyday conversation.

F The second revolutionary force is technology. Radio and television gave journalism the vivid immediacy it lacked. The blend of wireless telephony, the World Wide Web, and the miniaturisation of personal technology has helped to create a glut of news.

G But if it is the case that anyone can be a journalist, what is journalism? Whatever the era and technology, it must surely involve an organised attempt to show what is happening, to reduce or eliminate doubt about what is true.

Part 1

Look at the exam task. Quickly read the text without filling the gaps and answer these questions.

1 Who will be affected by the new law?
2 How long could offenders be sent to prison for?
3 Who was intimidated by paparazzi in the text?

Exam task

For questions **1–8**, read the text below and decide which answer (**A**, **B**, **C** or **D**) best fits each gap.
There is an example at the beginning (**0**).

Example:

0   **A** people   **B** figures   **C** citizens   **D** celebrities

New law to protect children from paparazzi

Paparazzi who harass the children of public (**0**) ..B... will face stiffer penalties under new legislation in California. The law signed by state governor Jerry Brown, increases (**1**) .... for actions that include taking photographs or videos of a child without consent. Media organisations had opposed the move, which increases penalties for harassing children because of their parents' job, on the (**2**) .... that it could restrict legitimate newsgathering activities. Those caught (**3**) .... the restrictions now (**4**) .... a maximum sentence of one year in jail and a fine of up to $10,000. The bill was given a boost when Hollywood actor Halle Berry gave it her (**5**) .... She said her daughter had been (**6**) ...... by aggressive photographers who followed them daily, often shouting as they (**7**) ...... images of the star and her family. Welcoming the legislation, she said: 'I started this fight with a great deal of hope and a bit of uncertainty so I am very (**8**) ...... to Governor Brown for recognising the plight of children who are tormented because of their parents' identity.'

1	**A** conclusions	**C** judgements
	B results	**D** penalties
2	**A** grounds	**C** arguments
	B reasons	**D** bases
3	**A** dismissing	**C** ignoring
	B opposing	**D** neglecting
4	**A** face	**C** meet
	B confront	**D** encounter
5	**A** encouragement	**C** support
	B help	**D** assistance
6	**A** afraid	**C** nervous
	B feared	**D** frightened
7	**A** captured	**C** grasped
	B seized	**D** grabbed
8	**A** appreciative	**C** grateful
	B pleased	**D** gratified

Listening

Part 4

1 Look at the exam task instructions and answer these questions.

1 How many speakers will you hear?
2 What will they be talking about?
3 In each A–H list how many choices do not match any of the speakers?

2 🎧 **02** Now listen and do the exam task.

Exam task

You will hear five short extracts in which people are talking about dramatic situations they have been in.

While you listen you must complete both tasks.

TASK ONE
For questions **1–5,** choose from the list **(A–H)** the situation each speaker describes.

A a hurricane	Speaker 1	1
B a civil conflict	Speaker 2	2
C a murder attempt		
D a domestic burglary	Speaker 3	3
E a vehicle fire	Speaker 4	4
F a motorway collision		
G a political resignation	Speaker 5	5
H unwanted press attention		

TASK TWO
For questions **6–10,** choose from the list **(A–H)** how each speaker felt in the situation they describe.

A amazed	Speaker 1	6
B unsurprised		
C anxious	Speaker 2	7
D terrified		
E embarrassed	Speaker 3	8
F shocked	Speaker 4	9
G apprehensive		
H lucky	Speaker 5	10

Grammar

Revision of verb tenses

1 Choose the correct verbs in these sentences.

1 If *I knew / I'd known* you were home, I'd have called you.
2 Police are *currently looking / currently look* into the accident.
3 This time next year, *I'll be studying / I'll have been studying* here for three years.
4 I tried to put my car into reverse gear while *I drive / I was driving* at 50 kph. The gears *made / have made* a dreadful noise.
5 By the time *we arrived / we've arrived* home, *we drove / we'd driven* 500 km.
6 I need to get fit, so I've decided *I'll start / I'm going to start* running every day.
7 It's a difficult question, but I'm sure *I know / I'm knowing* the answer.
8 *I just finished / I've just finished* writing an essay and *I'm / I'm being* exhausted.

2 Complete these sentences with the correct form of the verbs in brackets.

1 I'll go back to work when my child .... (*be*) one year old.
2 By the end of this decade most people .... (*forget*) many forms of entertainment from last century.
3 This movie .... (*download*) for ages. I need a faster connection!
4 This is the third book in the series they .... (*publish*) and I hear they .... (*bring out*) two more in March next year.
5 By the time the papers picked up the story it .... (*be*) all over social media sites for hours.

3 ⊘ Correct the verb tense mistakes made by exam candidates in these sentences.

1 I didn't met any other people apart from English people in our group.
2 Those were expenses that we didn't considered because we knew about them from the start.
3 The quality of the service were really unsatisfactory, giving me the impression that I joined a cheap holiday trip.
4 As I have started turning over the pages, I had some concerns.
5 Our International Students' Sports Club has being incredibly successful so far.

Writing

Part 1 Exam task: essay

Contrast links

1 Use the expressions in the box to complete the sentences.

> despite   in contrast   in spite of the fact that
> nevertheless

1 Many young people are well qualified. .... this, unemployment rates remain high.
2 Salaries and employment levels remain high for those over fifty. .... unemployment rates for those under twenty are incredibly high.
3 .... many people work, the cost of living continues to rise and poverty levels increase.
4 Living standards have been rising for decades. .... many still face challenging economic times.

2 Look at this exam task and answer these questions.

1 How many ways of dealing with the problem should you discuss?
2 Do you have to use the opinions from the discussion?

Your class has attended a panel discussion on the problem of youth unemployment and possible solutions to the problem. You have made the notes below.

> **Ways of dealing with the problem**
> - Retirement
> - Education
> - Skills
>
> Some opinions expressed in the discussion:
>
> "Young people should study practical subjects."
>
> "People should retire earlier."
>
> "All young people should have to get some qualifications."
>
> Write an essay for your tutor discussing **two** of the ideas in your notes. You should **explain which approach you think would be more effective, giving reasons** to support your opinion.
> You may, if you wish, make use of the opinions expressed in the discussion, but you should use your own words as far as possible.

3 Use the contrast links in the box to complete the essay on the right.

> However   Although   Despite   Nevertheless

Unemployment in many countries is at record levels; in particular, youth unemployment is almost out of control. It could even be argued that we are in danger of having a lost generation if urgent action is not taken. **(1)** ...., should effective policies be implemented, the consequences of this potential disaster could be minimised.

The first approach that could be taken is to raise the level of compulsory education. **(2)** .... this approach might cause financial problems for governments, this would probably cost no more than unemployment benefits. Raising academic standards and the level of skills training will enable the country as a whole to benefit from an improved range of skills.

Secondly, not only should education levels be raised for all, but the introduction of more relevant, practical and useful skills would also be beneficial for the country. Arguably, a significant proportion of today's youth have qualifications and skills that are held by too many people. **(3)** .... many young people gaining high level qualifications, the lack of diversification means that they are still faced with an uncertain career path as many of their skills are not those most in demand.

Reform of the education system would be costly and it is perhaps questionable whether the minimum level for all will address the issue. **(4)** .... raising awareness of the skills and qualifications our country is in desperate need of, would go some way to addressing the problem.

4 Now read this exam task and write an essay in **220–260** words in an appropriate style.

Your class has attended a panel discussion on the problem of long term unemployment among people over 50 and possible solutions to the problem. You have made the notes below.

> **Ways of dealing with the problem**
> - Retraining
> - Early retirement
> - Job sharing
>
> Some opinions expressed in the discussion:
>
> "The retirement age should be 55."
>
> "It's more important for young people to have jobs."
>
> "Job sharing should be encouraged."
>
> Write an essay for your tutor discussing **two** of the ideas in your notes. You should **explain which way of dealing with the problem you think would be more effective, giving reasons** to support your opinion.
> You may, if you wish, make use of the opinions expressed in the discussion, but you should use your own words as far as possible.

Reading and Use of English

Part 6

1 Look at the exam task and answer these questions.

   1 What is the topic of the four texts?
   2 In general, what do the questions ask you to look for in the texts?

Exam task

You are going to read four blogs about travel. For questions 1–4, choose from texts A–D. The blogs may be chosen more than once.

Travel today

Four travel bloggers give their opinion on the purpose of travel in the 21st century.

A
Arrival at a destination is often thought to be the prime purpose of travel these days. Taken in this way the journey itself is not the point, rather it is the serious business of transporting our bodies from one place to another. Getting to the end location as quickly as possible is the requirement and nowadays this is possible almost instantaneously. The modern method of travel seals us into tubes called aeroplanes as they charge through the sky at such speeds that we can hardly have any notion of the glorious planet we pass across. We want to get somewhere new and different as quickly as possible, and this is ironic as the very thing that enables us to get there quicker is also what makes all the "theres" so similar. Globalisation through airpower means stepping into the plane and swapping one city for another as though by some magic trick.

B
It is only since flying became the most popular means of long-distance travel for both leisure and business purposes that journeys have ceased to be of intrinsic interest to the majority of those travelling. In the past, when our only travel choices for such journeys were rail, sea or road, journeys themselves had to be taken account of. A journey that might have taken several days passing through different landscapes and climate zones, can now be completed in a few hours. Our place of arrival will, in many instances, be identical to our place of departure. This change has intellectual as well as practical implications. While we no longer need to worry about food, accommodation or changes of clothing during today's journeys, we are no longer in a position to enjoy the geographical and cultural differences between the places we pass through on our journeys. This is a serious loss.

C
There are those for whom travel is an end itself, a minority, in my opinion, who enjoy the journey to their destination more than their arrival. These people might deliberately choose a sea voyage lasting two weeks in preference to a long-haul flight. In my view, these travellers belong to a generation of romantics from a bygone age. Sadly, the many cultural differences that once characterised our world and made it a fascinating place to travel through have now all but disappeared. Why would a serious traveller choose to spend more of his or her time and probably money than is necessary simply to get from A to B? Whether one is going on an exotic holiday or an important business trip, the less time spent travelling the better for most modern travellers, especially as this means more time is spent at the chosen destination.

D
Those who travel through multiple time zones at high speed but do not realise that it is the journey, rather than the destination, that matters miss the opportunity to experience something very important. By stopping focusing on arriving, and by travelling long enough to feel the passage of time, we can come to realise that what really matters in travel is the same for life in general. That bubble all around us, that threatens always to trap us in the same frustration-coma we feel at home, can and must be resisted. Travel can and must become a joy in itself and then the broken down buses, the flies and the baking heat will not bother us. The evidence that this is possible is out there to see. Great travel books and writing are never just about the destination, they are about the changes the act of travelling bring about during a journey.

Which blogger

shares A's opinion about the relative importance of a journey and the arrival at a destination? **1** ☐

has a different opinion from the others about the cultural value of travel? **2** ☐

shares B's opinion about the kind of places people travel from and to? **3** ☐

takes a similar view to D on what we lose if we travel by air? **4** ☐

Grammar

Participle clauses

1 Rewrite these sentences using participle clauses.

   1 Because he was pleased with their behaviour, James took his children to a park.
     Pleased with the children's behaviour, James took them to a park.

   2 The new mall, which is located in the suburbs, is very popular.

   3 He was late for college yesterday, so he set his alarm for an earlier time this morning.

   4 After he had completed the project, he started his next venture.

   5 As she looked over her shoulder, she saw the train leaving.

   6 Because I had taken the wrong train, I found myself in Swindon not Oxford.

   7 The man who is walking the dog is a friend of mine.

   8 I didn't have a break all day, so I was desperate for something to eat.

   9 The presenter stepped up to the microphone. He cleared his voice.

  10 As long as you drive carefully, this car is quite safe.

2 Join these sentences using participle clauses.

   1 I have seen some of the damage done by tourists. I'm now a strong believer in eco-tourism.

   2 Eco-tourists want to boost the economies of the places they visit. They try to eat only locally produced food.

   3 The group arrived two hours late. They missed their flight.

   4 Mario is an experienced travel guide. He always gives reliable advice about places worth visiting.

   5 Uluru, or Ayers Rock, in Australia is now seriously eroded. It was climbed by large numbers of tourists.

   6 The Australian government gave Uluru back to the Aboriginal people in 1985. The government hoped that tourists would respect its spiritual significance.

Reading and Use of English

Part 3

Prefixes

1 Choose the correct words in these sentences.

   1 This option is *inappropriate / unappropriate* considering the choices available.
   2 The government has plans to *deregulate / disregulate* the banking system.
   3 It isn't always easy for the police to *enforce / inforce* speed limits.
   4 It's highly *unprobable / improbable* that they will agree.
   5 On that occasion, her behaviour was completely *irrrational / unrational*.

2 Complete the words in bold in these sentences with the appropriate prefix from the box.

anti	bi	inter	mis	out	over	re	under

   1 Can you …**call** what happened last night?
   2 Low-level crime which is not serious enough for a prison sentence is often referred to as …**social** behaviour.
   3 Communication at the college is poor. There's hardly any …**action** between the students and teachers.
   4 You did really well, definitely …**performing** most of the class. You might even have come first.
   5 You shouldn't …**estimate** the cost. It could be a lot more expensive than you think.
   6 Ben needs to calm down. He's getting …**excited**.
   7 The journal is …**annual**. It comes out in March and September.
   8 I prefer to speak on the phone. It's so easy to …**interpret** emails.

3 Look at the exam task instructions and quickly read the text. What did the writer see when she arrived in Phnom Penh?

Exam task

For questions **1–8**, read the text below. Use the word given in capitals at the end of some of the lines to form a word that fits in the gap **in the same line**. There is an example at the beginning (**0**).

Example: (**0**) RELATIVELY

My first solo trip

I am (**0**) .... well-travelled, but until now I have never really travelled alone. It was something that I needed to do. Sitting on the riverfront in Phnom Penh on my last night, I had to admit to feeling a sense of (**1**) .... It was a strange feeling leaving the (**2**) .... and companionship of my tour group and setting out on my own: a new (**3**) .... scene to adjust to, new towns to find my way around. But I soon realised that I was not alone. The Cambodian people are so (**4**) .... welcoming and friendly, and I met many (**5**) .... travellers along the way. I travelled by speed boat up the Mekong River, passing through border checkpoints. (**6**) ...., one of the first things we saw as we arrived in Phnom Penh was a New Zealand flag. After being (**7**) .... by a dishonest taxi driver, I arrived at Kambuja Inn – my home and (**8**) .... oasis for the next few days.

RELATE

ACCOMPLISH
SECURE

CULTURE

CREDIBLE
AGREE

SURPRISE

CHARGE

PEACE

Listening
Part 2

Do the exam task. Write no more than three words for each answer.

Exam task

🎧 **03** You will hear a student called Tom Sadler talking about a trip to The Galapagos Islands. For questions **1–8**, complete the sentences with a word or short phrase

Tom's visit to the Galapagos Islands

Tom's visit made him realise why Darwin had been (**1**) .... by the Galapagos Islands.

Before going there, Tom believed the islands were between Indonesia and (**2**) ....

Tom didn't have time to travel to the islands (**3**) ....

Santa Cruz was the (**4**) .... of Tom's trip.

Tom was very surprised to find jungle and (**5**) .... landscapes on the same island.

Tom regretted not taking an (**6**) .... with him when he went diving.

Instead of giving a detailed account, Tom lists some of the (**7**) .... of his visit.

The dolphins Tom saw on the last night of his trip appeared to (**8**) ....

Writing

Part 2 Exam task: report

1 ◉ Correct any errors you can see in these sentences.

1 To summing up, what we must do is encourage the next generation to do sports.

2 It also includes recommendation for improvements to help the department operate efficiently.

3 Despite the problems I outlines, I enjoyed attending this conference.

4 Shortly, everything's organised for you.

5 In order to considering appointing someone as my assistant, you have asked me to write this report outlining my needs.

6 The purpose of this report is suggesting the most suitable catering company.

7 All the above considered, I believe that my proposal meets your requirements.

8 I'd like to suggest you some improvements to the week's programme.

2 Read the exam task below and answer these questions.

1 What must you write about?
2 Who are you writing for and why do they want a report?
3 What points must you include?

> In your Geography class, you have been discussing the impact of tourism. Your tutor has asked you to write a report on a tourist region in your country.
> Your report should describe the place and say why it is popular, say what impact tourism has had on the region, and suggest changes that would improve the region.
>
> Write your **report**.

3 Quickly read the model report, Tourism in Cancun, and answer the questions.

1 Is the report organised into clear sections?
2 Is it written in an appropriate style?
3 What suggestions has the writer made?

Tourism in Cancun

The aim of this report is to provide information on the impact of the tourist industry on Cancun, a city located on the eastern coast of Mexico.

Tourists are attracted to Cancun for many reasons: its white sandy beaches, its bright blue waters, and its lagoon where many native species live. It has always been recognised as a beautiful place. It was known to the ancient Mayan tribes but when the government decided to develop the region in the 1970s, it expanded at an incredibly rapid rate. Its tropical climate varies very little from season to season and this means that visitor numbers are high throughout the year.

With regard to the impact tourism has had on this coastal city, the population, which numbered only a handful when construction began, has increased dramatically and the resort's rapid growth as a tourist destination has had negative environmental consequences. Parts of the lagoon have been destroyed or contaminated by the construction of a major highway system. A nearby rainforest has shrunk in size and the building of many hotels and restaurants has severely affected the natural habitats of local wildlife.

While it is true that Cancun is a prosperous tourist resort which provides employment for thousands of people, the impact its development has had on the environment is undeniable. For this reason, I would suggest that the government takes measures to reverse some of the damage that has been done. I would also suggest that businesses are encouraged to introduce more environmentally friendly practices.

4 Find sentences in paragraphs two and three which give the following information:

- The historical background
- The effect on the original town
- The reason for its popularity
- Specific examples of the impact

5 Write your own report in answer to the same exam task. Choose a tourist destination in your country that you know about. Write 220–260 words in an appropriate style.

3 Behaving and interacting

Reading and Use of English

Part 5 Exam task

You are going to read a text about the impact of social media. For questions **1–6**, choose the answer (**A**, **B** ,**C**, or **D**) which you think fits best according to the text.

The Impact of Social Media on Children, Adolescents, and Families

Engaging in social media is a routine activity that has been shown to benefit young people by enhancing communication and social skills. Social media sites such as Facebook offer multiple opportunities for connecting with friends and people with shared interests. In recent years, the number of young people using such sites has increased dramatically, with many logging on more than ten times a day. In addition, a large proportion of teenagers now own mobile phones, so a large part of their social and emotional development is occurring while they are on the Internet or on mobiles.

Because of their limited capacity for self-regulation and susceptibility to peer pressure, young people are at some risk as they experiment with social media. Research indicates that there are frequent online expressions of offline behaviours, such as bullying and clique-forming, that have introduced problems such as cyberbullying. Other problems that merit awareness include internet addiction.

Many parents today use technology incredibly well and feel comfortable with the programs and online venues that their children are using. Nevertheless, for various reasons, some may find it difficult to relate to their digitally smart youngsters. Such parents may lack a basic understanding of these forms of socialisation, which are integral to children's lives. Frequently, they do not have the technical abilities or time needed to keep pace with their children in their ever-changing internet habits. In addition, these parents often lack a basic understanding that children's online lives are an extension of their offline lives. The result can be a knowledge and skill gap, which creates a disconnect in how these parents and their children relate.

Social media sites allow young people to accomplish online many of the tasks that are important to them offline: staying connected with friends and family, making new friends, and exchanging ideas. Older students also use social media to connect with one another on school work. For example, Facebook allows students to gather outside class to exchange ideas about assignments. Some schools successfully use blogs as teaching tools, which has the benefit of reinforcing skills in written expression and creativity. Adolescents are also finding that they can access online information about their health concerns easily and anonymously. Excellent health resources are increasingly available to youth on topics such as stress reduction. However, because of their young age, adolescents can encounter inaccuracies during these searches and may require parental involvement to be sure they are using reliable online resources, interpreting the information correctly, and not becoming overwhelmed by what they are reading.

Using social media becomes a risk to adolescents more often than adults realise. Most risks fall into these categories: peer-to-peer; lack of understanding of online privacy issues; and the influences of advertisers. Although "online harassment" is often used interchangeably with the term "cyberbullying", it is actually different. Research suggests that online harassment is not as common as offline harassment, and participation in social networking sites does not put most children at risk of online harassment. Cyberbullying is deliberately using digital media to communicate false, embarrassing, or hostile information about another person. It is the most common online risk for all teens, and can have profound emotional effects.

Researchers have proposed a new phenomenon called "Facebook depression", defined as depression that develops when youngsters spend a great deal of time on social media sites and then begin to exhibit classic symptoms of depression. The intensity of the online world is thought to be a factor that may trigger depression in some adolescents. As with offline depression, young people who suffer from Facebook depression are at risk of social isolation and sometimes turn to risky internet sites for "help". The main risks to young people online today are each other, risks of improper use of technology, lack of privacy, or posting false information about themselves or others. These types of behaviour endanger their privacy.

When people go onto websites, they can leave evidence of their visits. This ongoing record of online activity is called the "digital footprint". One of the biggest threats to young people on social media sites is to their digital footprint and future reputations. Young people who lack an awareness of privacy issues often post inappropriate material without understanding that "what goes online stays online". As a result, future jobs and college acceptance may be put in jeopardy by inexperienced clicks of the mouse.

1 How does the writer explain why young people could face some problems when they use social media?
A They spend more time than they should on social media sites.
B They cannot control their use of social media sites well enough.
C They are unaware of the ways in which others use social media sites.
D Their use of social media sites and mobile phones has increased.

2 The writer suggests that there is a problem between parents and their children because parents
A do not understand the technology behind social media sites.
B take little interest in their children's online behaviour.
C feel excluded from their children's online lives.
D do not understand the relationship between children's online and offline lives.

3 The writer suggests it may be dangerous for young people to access online health information because
A they can get information without saying who they are.
B the information they find may not be correct.
C they may refuse to share the information they find with their parents.
D they may not be able to find the information they need.

4 According to the writer, online harassment
A is another term for cyberbullying.
B is the most common danger facing internet users.
C affects a majority of young people.
D is not as frequent as real-life harassment.

5 In the sixth paragraph, the writer suggests that young social media users who feel socially excluded may
A give away more personal information than they should.
B be at risk of becoming seriously depressed.
C look for advice and support on unreliable websites.
D tell lies about themselves and other people.

6 The writer uses the term 'digital footprint' to refer to
A a permanent account of someone's contributions to a social media site.
B a list of places someone has visited.
C the information that someone wishes to keep private.
D a record of jobs and college places someone has applied for.

Part 4

Look at the exam task and answer these questions about each item.

1 Which part of speech is the key word?
2 Which part/s of the first sentence must you replace?

Exam task

For questions **1–6**, complete the second sentence so that it has a similar meaning to the first sentence, using the word given. **Do not change the word given.** You must use between **three** and **six** words, including the word given. Here is an example (**0**).

Example:

0 Sam has constantly attempted not to attract attention since the trial began.
PROFILE
Sam has made constant ATTEMPTS TO KEEP A LOW PROFILE since the trial began.

1 He ignored the 'do not enter' sign and went straight in.
ATTENTION
He didn't .... the 'do not enter' sign and went straight in.

2 She wishes she had accepted the job offer.
TURNING
She .... of the job.

3 He failed to persuade her not to resign.
TALKED
She couldn't be ....

4 The exam was so long he just couldn't continue to concentrate at such a high level.
KEEP
He couldn't .... of concentration needed for such a long exam.

5 'Why don't we get together for a chat tomorrow afternoon?' Rosie said.
MEETING
Rosie .... for a chat the following afternoon.

6 You won't achieve anything if you refuse to talk to him.
POINT
There's .... to talk to him.

Listening

Look at the exam task and answer this question for each extract. Then do the task.

Who will you hear and what will they talk about?

Exam task

🎧 **04** You will hear three different extracts. For questions **1–6**, choose the answer (**A**, **B** or **C**) which fits best according to what you hear. There are two questions for each extract.

Extract One

You hear two friends discussing an article they have both read.

1 The article they are discussing focused on
  A the importance of rewarding good behaviour.
  B the way people make decisions.
  C the way the human brain functions.

2 What was the most interesting thing for the woman?
  A Teenagers are extremely reluctant to take risks.
  B Teenagers tend to be more decisive than adults.
  C Education can slow the speed at which teenagers develop mentally.

Extract Two

You hear two students discussing a group presentation they have to give.

3 What problem are the students discussing?
  A The third person in the group is not taking part.
  B They have not started their presentation.
  C They have not had enough time to practise.

4 The students both expect
  A to get no practical help from their tutor.
  B their tutor to make useful suggestions.
  C their tutor to insist that they work as a team.

Extract Three

You hear two friends talking about living alone.

5 They both think that living alone is
  A preferable in every respect to sharing.
  B dull compared with having flatmates.
  C an unnatural way of living.

6 During their conversation, the man admits that he
  A is an unsociable person.
  B is thinking of moving again.
  C took something that did not belong to him.

Grammar

Reported speech

1 Match the reporting verbs in the box to the patterns below. More than one pattern may be possible.

accept admit advise agree argue complain convince deny explain inform persuade promise remind suggest tell warn

1 verb + *that*	
2 verb + object + *that*	
3 verb + *to* infinitive	
4 verb + object + *to* + infinitive	
5 verb + *ing*	

2 Read these statements from the recording and rewrite them as reported speech. Use a range of reporting verbs.

1 I can really relate to that. (Rita)
  Rita agreed that ....

2 I just need to finish off the bibliography. (Hannah)
....

3 He'll just say that's one of the challenges of teamwork. (Hannah)
....

4 Let's get in touch with Nick again. (Tom)
....

5 I haven't got used to the lack of atmosphere with no other flatmates. (Anthony)
....

6 I can spend days not seeing someone else. (Anthony)
....

7 You used to love living in our house. (Anthony)
....

3 Rewrite these questions in reported speech using the words in brackets.

1 What do you think the weather's going to be like tomorrow. (Ben → Hannah – ask)
  Ben asked Hannah what ....

2 Can you lend me some money until next week? (Scott → Peter – want to know)
....

3 Did you watch the match last night? (John → Ed – ask)
....

4 Has anyone seen my mobile phone? (Tom – wonder)
....

5 What time will you be home tonight. (Maria → Juan – ask)
....

Writing

Part 2 Exam task: letter

Register

1 ⊙ The underlined words and phrases in these sentences written by exam candidates are too formal. Replace these words and phrases with more informal alternatives. (More than one answer may be possible.)

1 I think these are very rational <u>persons</u> who want to give everything a meaning.
2 I work all day and <u>thus cannot</u> spend much time with my children.
3 I am going to <u>participate</u> in a competition.
4 <u>Moreover</u>, they find the staff very unfriendly.
5 Citizens are overwhelmed by <u>large quantities of information</u>.
6 <u>We shall meet</u> at 3.30. Is that OK?

2 Look at this exam task and answer these questions.

1 Why has the friend written to "you"?
2 What is the main subject of the letter that "you" have to write?
3 What does the friend offer to do?

You are having problems at work with your boss and you mentioned this in a recent letter to an English-speaking friend. Here is part of your friend's reply.

So what exactly has your boss been doing? How does she treat the other staff? Why do you think she is so hard on you? Is there anything I can do to help?

Write your **letter**.

3 Read the model letter below ignoring the sections in italics for the moment. In which paragraph/s does the writer ...

1 describe the main issue?
2 apologise for the tone of the last letter?
3 answer the how question?
4 ask the reader for advice?
5 try to explain the boss's behaviour?

Dear Ruby,

Thanks for your letter – it's really good to hear from you. (1) *Please accept my apologies / I'm sorry* for complaining so much in the last letter but this situation has really (2) *got me down / depressed me.*

(3) *Basically / Fundamentally*, my manager has been making life very difficult for me. Ever since our (4) *disagreement / row* last week, she has been treating me differently. She always gives me the worst jobs, and is really strict about my timekeeping.

Some of the others take much longer breaks than they (5) *are supposed to / are entitled to*, but if I go over by just a couple of minutes she insists on having (6) *a discussion / a word* with me. Not only does she give the others longer breaks and easier jobs, she's always praising them and (7) *criticising me / putting me down*. She's negative about everything I do, and (8) *reprimands me / tells me off* me in front of my (9) *workmates / colleagues*. (10) *I dread / I am fearful of* going to work every day.

As I said, I get the (11) *feeling / impression* she is like this with me because of our recent argument, but I also think she has personal issues. She's quite ageist and I think it's even worse because I'm young. It's like I'm her child!

So what did your boss do? Was it similar? Any advice you've got would be great. I really don't know how to (12) *improve the situation / make things better*. If it wasn't for her, it would be a great place to work.

Hope to hear from you soon.

Best wishes

Paula

4 Read the letter again and choose the appropriate words and phrases in italics. Remember this is an informal letter to a friend.

5 Now read this exam task and write your letter in an appropriate style in **220–260** words.

For various reasons, you are finding it difficult at the moment to concentrate on your studies. You mentioned this in a recent letter to an English-speaking friend. Here is part of your friend's reply.

So what exactly is the problem? Are you having second thoughts about the subjects you have chosen, or are there other, perhaps more interesting things on your mind?

Write your **letter**.

Reading and Use of English

You are going to read a newspaper article about the link between money and happiness. Six paragraphs have been removed from the article. Choose from the paragraphs **A–G** the one which fits each gap (**1–6**). There is one extra paragraph which you do not need to use.

Money weakens our ability to enjoy life's little pleasures

There has long been a perceived link between money and happiness. Many people dream of the life they could lead if they won the lottery – a world of mansions, fine restaurants, and first-class travel. But few consider the costs. These fineries could lead to so much enjoyment that we would no longer be able to appreciate life's simpler pleasures, like a walk on a sunny day or the taste of a bar of chocolate.

1 [ ]

Jordi Quoidbach from the University of Liege showed that richer people aren't as good at appreciating everyday pleasures as poorer people. Even the mere thought of money can make us take mundane joys for granted. Normal people who were reminded about wealth spent less time appreciating a humble bar of chocolate and obtained less enjoyment from it.

2 [ ]

Perhaps this is because money both gives and takes away: it opens doors to new pleasures, while making delights that were already accessible seem less enticing. Obsessing over wealth is like being on a treadmill – continuously running to stay in the same place emotionally. To begin with, Quoidbach asked 351 university employees, from cleaners to senior staff, to complete a test that measured their ability to feel positive emotions. Each recruit was asked to put themselves in a detailed pleasant scenario, from finishing an important task to discovering an amazing waterfall on a hike.

3 [ ]

Using other questionnaires, Quoidbach also assessed how happy they were, how much money it would take to live their dream life. And as a final twist, half of the questionnaires included a picture of a large stack of euros, while the other half saw the same picture that had been

blurred beyond recognition. He found that the more money the recruits had, the worse they were at appreciating their positive emotions.

4 [ ]

In fact, the recruits also tended to be slightly happier the more money they had. Other studies have found the same trend, but Quoidbach's important result is that money would have had a far greater impact on the volunteers' happiness were it not for its negative effect on their ability to enjoy.

5 [ ]

Two researchers kept an eye on them and not only timed their eating, but rated how much enjoyment they were showing. The results were clear – the recruits who saw the money took 32 seconds to eat the chocolate, significantly less than the 45 seconds spent by the others. And on average, their happiness rating, as judged by the observers, was considerably lower than their peers.

6 [ ]

However, having money reduces the odds that people will actually spend it in this way! Dunn has also found that money is better used to buy happiness if it's spent on experiences rather than goods. In both experiments, a simple reminder of wealth weakened people's ability to appreciate life's smaller pleasures. That's a striking result and Quoidbach explains it best himself. "One need not actually visit the pyramids of Egypt or spend a week at the legendary Banff spas in Canada for one's ability to enjoy to be impaired," he writes. "Simply knowing that these peak experiences are readily available may increase one's tendency to take the small pleasures of daily life for granted."

A

Quoidbach found that a person's ability to appreciate was unrelated to their desire for money. And even suggesting the thought of money, by showing them the euro picture, had the same negative effect, dampening their reactions to the happy imaginings.

B

Moreover, the negative impact of wealth on individuals' ability to appreciate undermined the positive effects of money on their happiness. We experimentally exposed participants to a reminder of wealth and produced the same negative effect on their ability to enjoy as that produced by actual individual differences in wealth.

C

Of course, there's only so far you can take the results of these questionnaires. A more objective experiment would be better, and that's exactly what Quoidbach did. He asked 40 students to volunteer for a taste test. They were given a binder that included a questionnaire about their attitudes toward chocolate. On the opposite page, apparently for an unrelated study, was a picture of either money or a neutral object. Afterwards, all they had to do was eat a chocolate.

D

Quoidbach's study helps to make sense of a trend in psychological research, where money has an incredibly weak effect on happiness. Once people have enough to buy basic needs and rise out of poverty, having extra cash has little bearing on their enjoyment of life.

E

This idea of wealth as a double-edged sword is widely held and while it's easy to suggest that it springs from jealousy, a new set of experiments supports the idea.

F

These studies are part of a growing body of research showing that the link between money and happiness is more complicated than we might imagine. Elizabeth Dunn, who worked with Quoidbach, has previously shown that money can buy happiness if it's spent on others.

G

Afterwards, they were quizzed in detail about how they would react to the scenarios, to see how strongly they enjoyed the experiences.

Part 2 Exam task

For questions **1–8**, read the text below and think of the word which best fits each gap. Use only **one** word in each gap. There is an example at the beginning (**0**).
Example: (0) FIRST

Measuring success

Many countries regard income (**0**) .... and foremost (**1**) .... the primary means of determining their success in (**2**) .... with other countries. This measure divides the value of a country's annual production by the number of people resident in the country. In 1998, (**3**) .... , the King of Bhutan announced that in future his nation's main measure of success (**4**) .... be happiness rather than income. He did this with a view (**5**) .... showing the world that money does not equal happiness.

A year later, the king (**6**) .... the fateful decision to allow television into his country. Until then, it had been banned, as (**7**) .... all forms of advertising. But in 1999, TV sets began to be imported into the country and, as a (**8**) .... , people started to spend a lot of time watching television programmes. Around the same time, children began fighting more, crime increased and more married couples separated or divorced.

Vocabulary – Money

Complete these sentences with words from the box.

> break even   gross   incomes   interest   loss
> make ends meet   overdrawn   overheads   profit
> taxed   unaffordable

1 Many basic products are .... for people on lower .... Many of them really struggle to ....

2 My .... income, that's before tax, is only £20,000. It's not really enough for me to live on and so my account is constantly ....

3 I earn 2% .... on my savings, but then that is .... by the government at 20%.

4 She has a very successful business, but she is still always trying to reduce her ....

5 In the first few years, most companies make a .... and many don't .... until year three of trading. Only in year four do they actually start to make a ....

Grammar

Passive and causative verb forms

1 Rewrite the underlined parts of these sentences using passive verbs. Start your sentences with *It …* (You may include an agent in your sentences.).

1 <u>A report has proved</u> that shoplifting has increased every year since 2011.

....

2 <u>A new report will claim</u> that teenagers may become depressed if they spend too long on these sites.

....

3 <u>They say</u> that credit cards are not as easy to forge as they were a few years ago.

....

4 <u>People think</u> that the money was stolen while the shopkeeper was in his storeroom.

....

5 <u>Studies have shown</u> that teenagers are spending a lot of time on social media sites.

....

2 ⊘ Correct the mistakes in these sentences written by exam candidates. Not all of these sentences need passive verbs.

1 People's spending habits influence by different factors.

....

2 As you probably know, it is needed to have a good level of English in order to attend that university.

....

3 This custom is being disappeared lately.

....

4 England was qualified for the finals of the World Cup.

....

5 The story is being set in the 30s.

....

Listening

Part 3 Exam task

🎧 **05** You will hear an interview in which two journalists, Jonathan Wood and Laura Key, are discussing the subject of foreign aid to poor countries. For questions **1–6**, choose the answer (**A**, **B**, **C** or **D**) which fits best according to what you hear.

1 In Jonathan's opinion, most people in countries which give foreign aid
  A support their governments' gifts of aid to poor countries.
  B are happier giving to non-governmental organisations.
  C want their governments to spend more money at home.
  D are less generous that they were in the past.

2 Laura believes that the priority in most people's mind is
  A the honesty of the governments which receive the aid.
  B the amount of aid money that is given.
  C the way in which the use of aid money is checked.
  D the way in which aid money is used.

3 What practical use of aid money do both speakers refer to?
  A supporting agricultural projects
  B training for doctors and nurses
  C providing health facilities
  D providing educational support

4 Jonathan and Laura agree that most aid money should be spent
  A on long-term projects.
  B in donor countries.
  C on health projects.
  D on emergencies.

5 Laura's main objection to aid being linked to trade is that
  A it does not reach the people most in need.
  B it is sometimes used for military purposes.
  C it mainly benefits the donor country.
  D it is used by corrupt politicians.

6 Jonathan believes that aid linked to trade is beneficial as long as
  A it is all spent in the receiving countries.
  B politicians in the receiving countries are honest.
  C it provides employment in the receiving countries.
  D it is not used on security in the receiving countries.

Writing

Part 1 Exam task: essay

1 Read the exam task and model essay and answer these questions. (Ignore the gaps for the moment.)

1 Which two areas has the writer chosen to discuss?
2 What reasons have been given?
3 How have they paraphrased one of the opinions?

Your class has been watching a TV documentary about whether some advertising aimed at children should be banned. You have made the notes below.

Issues raised	Some opinions expressed in the discussion:
• children's health	"TV advertising puts pressure on parents to buy children things."
• demands on parents	"Children eat unhealthy food because of ads."
• role of government	"Advertisements distort a child's view of the world."

Write an essay for your tutor discussing **two** of the issues raised in your notes. You should **explain which issues are of most concern, giving reasons** to support your opinion.
You may, if you wish, make use of the opinions expressed in the discussion, but you should use your own words as far as possible.

Advertising has been blamed for many of the problems society faces. In particular, people are concerned about the impact advertising has on children. Obesity, (1) .... , is a growing concern, with many producers of unhealthy products specifically targeting younger consumers, who then may try to force their parents to buy these products.

A number of factors contribute to the obesity epidemic affecting young people, from inactive lifestyles (2) .... changing diets. There is also, (3) .... , concern about the impact of advertising. (4) .... , there are questions about the quality of the products being aimed at young people, (5) .... it is also the manner in which companies choose to promote their products that causes concern. Associating a product with a sport or a well-known athlete may give children the impression that a product is healthy, when (6) .... it is not.

(7) .... are there concerns about what is sold to children and how it is sold, but also about the growing influence children have over household spending. Advertising can lead to parents feeling obliged to give in to their children's unreasonable demands. (8) .... is the concern that some countries have taken the step of banning advertising to young children, or controlling more strictly the products that can be advertised on certain TV channels at particular times of day.

My (9) .... is that the physical health of children is a priority for society. I believe that there should be more controls over the advertising of certain products. (10) .... , I think advertising certain products to young children should be banned.

2 Complete the essay with words or phrases from the box.

> but   firstly   for example   to   however   in fact   in the end   not only   own view   such

3 Read this exam task and write your own essay in an appropriate style in **220–260 words**.

Your class has been having a discussion about how young people can be persuaded to save money regularly. You have made the notes below.

Ways of persuading people to save money

• attractive interest rates
• future needs
• reduce current spending

Some opinions expressed in the discussion:

"Most young people need all their income just to survive now."

"Young people find it difficult to do anything regularly."

"Young people prefer to enjoy themselves now rather than worry about the future."

Write an essay for your tutor discussing **two** of the methods of persuasion. **You should explain which area you think is more likely to be effective, giving reasons** to support your opinion.
You may, if you wish, make use of the opinions expressed in the discussion, but you should use your own words as far as possible.

Reading and Use of English

Part 8

Before doing the exam task, underline the key words or phrases in the questions.

Exam task

You are going to read a magazine article in which five people talk about their decision to run their first marathon. For questions **1–10**, choose from the five runners (**A–E**). The runners may be chosen more than once.

Which runner

decided not to be put off running because of a previous experience?	1
expected the preparation for running the marathon to be worse than it was?	2
found that the training programme seemed to go more quickly?	3
imagined that a previous injury would prevent them from competing?	4
intended to avoid walking as this might lead to a physical problem?	5
made the decision to run without weighing up the advantages and disadvantages?	6
simply wanted to complete a race however much time it took?	7
thought of the marathon as being a way of celebrating an important event?	8
was in good physical condition prior to starting their marathon preparation?	9
was motivated to run after watching the end of a marathon?	10

FIRST MARATHONS

A Susie Gordon

Susie enjoyed cycling as part of her daily routine. Then one year she went to support some friends who took part in a marathon, and was inspired. "I found it really moving to see all these people doing this amazing thing," she says. "They had trained for so long and this was their day. I wanted to experience that." She began a six-month training schedule. "The programme is designed to take you from a standing start to being able to run a marathon," says Susie. "The aim was to get you to have enough fitness and stamina to run a marathon with minimum risk of injury." Susie's healthy lifestyle and fitness were a good basis for the demanding training routine. Week one involved alternating short bursts of running with walking. "I was expecting the training to be awful, but it wasn't," says Susie.

B Ben Harrier

Looking back, the reasons I finally decided to 'take the plunge' and run a marathon are unclear. It was a snap decision really – I certainly didn't debate the pros and cons for long. There were many factors that led to my sudden decision. I'd always had some interest in running as a way to stay in shape, but every time I did too much too soon, I injured myself and did not want to continue. When I reached my mid-forties, I decided I had to get my act together – mentally and physically. I started walking, then inserted running intervals of a few hundred metres, then gradually extended the runs and reduced the walks until I was running two or three miles without a rest. I found this healthy and therapeutic, and something I was fairly good at.

C Vicky Lawrence

I started training for my first marathon in May after being inspired by a marathon in my home city. Witnessing all those people crossing the finish line made me want to sign up for a similar event. Initially it was just one more thing on my list of "things to do". I'd run one and then I'd be finished. I wanted to set a goal for myself and achieve it and didn't care how long it took. I just wanted to finish. So, I trained for months, running shorter routes during the week, and going on epic jaunts at weekends. Every Saturday was a new personal best in terms of distance achieved. My longest run was twenty miles. I tested out my race day clothes to make sure they were comfortable, and tried pre-race meals of oatmeal, peanut butter and a banana.

D   Jon Carter

Having torn a muscle at the beginning of the year, I thought I would never run again. To pick myself up after that was difficult and to hear people around me talking about the runs they were doing made me more miserable. Out of frustration, I signed up for a half marathon scheduled four months later. Amazingly, I managed to complete my first half marathon within the qualifying time. I was motivated. When it came the time to register for the November marathon, my husband said he wanted to do the full marathon. It coincided with our first wedding anniversary and he said that he would run for us. I thought, "Why not?" I would complete a full marathon for us, too.

E   Sally Woods

The sixteen weeks before the race seemed to go really slowly at first. Then the weeks flew by. My weekly mileage started climbing and I continued to be injury-free. But the work got harder as the runs got longer and more like real marathon training. I began to tell people that I was planning to run a marathon. 'Where?' They'd ask. 'In the park,' I'd say. 'Have you ever done one before?' they'd ask. 'No,' I said, 'so I have no idea what I'm in for, which is just the way I want it.' I prepared myself as best I could. I formulated a nutrition plan. I determined that I was going to run for as long as I could, as I have knee problems when I start running again after a walk.

Part 3

Suffixes

1   Put the following words in the correct lists according to their suffix.

activity archaeologist attractive awful certainly comfortable dangerous decision friendly friendship frustration healthy hopeless hospitalise kindness lengthen medical mentally mentor modernise modify nutrition obviously participant qualify sharpen therapeutic

Noun	Verb	Adjective	Adverb

2   Look at the exam task and decide how you have to change the words in capitals so that they fit correctly into the text. In the example, *science* is a noun changed to a different plural noun.

Exam task

For questions **1–8**, read the text below. Use the word given in capitals at the end of some of the lines to form a word that fits in the gap **on the same line**. There is an example at the beginning. **(0)**

Example: **(0)** SCIENTISTS

A cure for the common cold

A team of research **(0)** .... from university medical departments in Europe, China and Australia are working to neutralise a group of viruses known to be **(1)** .... for the sometimes **(2)** .... hand, foot and mouth disease which is common throughout Asia. They recently made a **(3)** .... breakthrough when they discovered a substance which can **(4)** .... viruses in such a way that they become completely **(5)** .... to humans. The substance affects the structure of the virus and prevents it from breaking up and infecting humans.
The team now believe they will soon succeed in devising an **(6)** .... way of eliminating the common cold – a virus for which there is currently no cure. Although their work is still at an early stage, members of the group are **(7)** .... about their chances of eventual success. If the international team succeed, millions of people across the world will be eternally grateful because it means they will no longer have to suffer the **(8)** .... associated with the common cold.

SCIENCE
RESPOND
DEAD
REMARK
WEAK
HARM
EFFECT
OPTIMIST
COMFORT

Listening

Vocabulary – Word building

1   Use the word in capitals to form a word that fits in the gap in each sentence.

1   Most doctors believe that
.... is preferable to cure.   **PREVENT**

2   A new vaccine is currently undergoing
.... trials.   **CLINIC**

3   A general anaesthetic is not needed
for most minor ....   **SURGEON**

4   At no time during the operation did
the patient lose ....   **CONSCIOUS**

5   Thanks to effective ....
care, the infection was cured.   **MEDICINE**

2   Read sentences 1–8 below and think about the kind of information which is missing. Now do the exam task.

Exam task

🎧 **06**   You will hear Phil Matthews, a medical student, giving a presentation to fellow students about a member of his family with diabetes. For questions 1–8, complete the sentences with a word or short phrase.

Living with diabetes

The lectures on diabetes have been **(1)** ....
for Phil because his father has recently learned he has the disease.

In addition to dizziness and general weakness,
(2) .... is a symptom of low blood sugar.

In Phil's opinion, simply telling his father to
(3) .... was not sufficient advice.

On finding out he had diabetes, Phil's father felt
(4) .... as well as shock.

Diabetes is a **(5)** .... disease which
means that it gets gradually worse over time.

Phil was not surprised that his father started by trying the
(6) .... method of controlling his
diabetes.

Doing anything **(7)** .... makes Phil's
father feel sleepy quite quickly.

Phil is **(8)** .... to do everything he can to
avoid developing diabetes himself.

Grammar

Conditional forms

1   Complete these sentences with the correct form of the verbs in brackets.

1   If he .... the doctor's advice, he'd
probably have diabetes now. (*not take*)

2   You'll be able to get an appointment as long as you
.... the surgery before 8.00 in the
morning. (*phone*)

3   If I were you, I .... for a second
opinion. (*ask*)

4   She .... alive now if the paramedics
hadn't arrived so quickly. (*be*)

5   You've been ill, so don't go out unless it
.... absolutely essential. (*be*)

6   If he hadn't broken his leg last week, he
.... football tomorrow. (*play*)

2   Complete the second of each pair of sentences so that it has the same meaning as the first. Start with the words given.

1   You will lose weight provided you stick to your calorie-controlled diet.
If you don't stick ....

2   I wouldn't go to the doctor unless I felt really ill.
Only if I felt really ill, ...

3   I went to the dentist yesterday afternoon, so I didn't lose my tooth.
I'd have lost my tooth ....

4   You'll stay fit and healthy as long as you take regular exercise.
Provided you ....

5   Because he kept to a healthy diet, he was rarely ill.
He would have been ill more frequently ....
....

Writing

Part 2 Exam task: proposal

Purpose and reason links

1 Complete these sentences with the correct linking words or phrases from the list. Sometimes more than one answer is possible.

> because   because of   due to   in order to
> so   so as not to   so as to   so that   to

1 The doctor prescribed tablets .... help reduce the patient's cholesterol levels.
2 Obesity is largely .... overeating and lack of exercise.
3 My brother started going to the gym .... he could become fit again after his operation.
4 You need to eat slowly .... make sure you digest your food properly.
5 Jorge is training every day .... he's running a marathon at the weekend.
6 They closed the door quietly .... wake their parents.
7 Hospitals are cleaned several times a day .... stop the spread of infections.
8 We couldn't go running yesterday .... the snow.

2 Read the exam task and decide on three section headings in addition to the *Introduction* and *Conclusion*.

> You see this notice in a local newspaper of the town where you are living.
>
> The Government has promised extra money to improve health facilities in the town. The Minister for Health is inviting people living in the town to send in proposals saying which facility or facilities should receive the money, how this should be spent and how this spending would benefit people in the town.
>
> Write your **proposal**.

3 Quickly read the model proposal and tick any points you agree with. Has the writer used the same or similar section headings to you?

Proposal for improved health facilities

Introduction

The (1) <u>aim</u> of this proposal is to (2) <u>suggest</u> the most suitable way of spending the money the government is providing for improving the town's health services.

A new hospital

The town's hospital is now over forty years old. Since it was built, the population of the town has doubled in size. (3) <u>This means</u> that the hospital sometimes finds it difficult to meet local demand, and patients (4) <u>frequently</u> have to travel to neighbouring towns for hospital treatment.

Protecting future generations

Everyone in the town would (5) <u>benefit</u> from a larger, more modern hospital, but children and young people would probably benefit most, (6) <u>as</u> the town's growing population includes many families with small children. (7) <u>For this reason</u>, it would be sensible to channel money into building new children's wards and a new maternity block. It is (8) <u>currently</u> (9) <u>not uncommon</u> for mothers to have to go to a hospital more than 40 kilometres away to have their babies. In emergencies, this can cause (10) <u>problems</u>.

Reassuring the population

(11) <u>At the moment</u>, there is some anxiety among parents that when their children are ill, they may not be receiving the best possible care. Fortunately, there have been very few bad experiences, and the doctors and nurses here do an excellent job. However, new children's and maternity facilities would, I believe, reassure people that the hospital offers their children the best possible care.

Conclusion

I would strongly recommend that the government money is spent on a new maternity block and improved facilities for children and young people.

4 Suggest alternatives for the underlined words in the proposal.

5 Now read the following exam task and write your own proposal in an appropriate style in **220–260** words.

> You see this notice in a local newspaper of the town where you are living.
>
> The Government has promised extra money to help reduce road accidents in the town where you are living. The Minister for Transport is inviting people living in the town to send in proposals saying how they think road accidents can be reduced or prevented. You will need to justify your opinions.
>
> Write your **proposal**.

Reading and Use of English

You are going to read a magazine article. For questions 1–6, choose the answer (A, B, C or D) which you think fits best according to the text.

Who owns the networked future of reading?

Some years ago, I came across a battered copy of *The Silence of the Lambs* in a train carriage. It was during one of those lonely chunks of life when reading takes on a new importance, and I found a quite unexpected friend in that rather dark and worrying tale. The anonymous former owner had done little drawings and written notes in the margins of the book before inexplicably leaving it on public transport. Amusing, insightful and often unrelated to the actual text, the previous reader's commentary entirely changed my reading of Thomas Harris's story of a serial murderer and obsessive police procedure.

My anonymous guide was a university student, most likely a young woman, studying the book from a feminist point of view. Harris's novel is a superior police procedural, but still guilty of that genre's casual sexism, picked apart by my guide with glee.

I've often wished that I could talk to that anonymous commentator. Today, if they were using an e-reader, I might be able to by using *Readmill*, an e-reading app that, on the surface at least, will be familiar to anyone who has read a book on their smartphone or tablet. But what makes this particular app a potential best-seller is how it helps readers – and writers – talk to each other.

One of the world's most popular e-readers Amazon's Kindle, lets readers see which sections of a text have been underlined most frequently by other readers: a frustrating feature given what could be achieved. Amazon also provides a social network app for readers, but shows no sign of integrating it into its ebooks. And it seems that the Kindle is unlikely to ever truly embrace the power of networks.

The app *Readmill* aims to fulfil the potential of networked reading. Readers can underline and comment on a text as much as they like, then open up those comments for discussion among a growing community of passionate readers. It's a simple but powerful feature that could be a serious threat to Kindle technology.

But this is only the leading edge of the networked reading revolution. *Readmill* allows authors to claim ownership of their books, and interact with readers in the margins of the text. So not only could I and my anonymous commentator debate the feminist critique of *The Silence of the Lambs* but, should he feel so inspired, Thomas Harris himself could respond, in a conversation directly related to the text itself.

To understand what a fully realised network reading experience might mean, imagine reading a book published in 2013 in the year 2063. In the 50 years between these two dates, dozens of critical texts, hundreds of articles, thousands of reviews and hundreds of thousands of comments will have been made on the text. In a fully networked reading experience, all of those will be available to the reader of the book from within the text.

Authors are able to shape the discussion on their books; they can maintain a relationship with all the readers who have enjoyed their books, whether that is a few dozen or a few hundred million. And perhaps most interesting of all, readers can find each other through the books they read. In a world of seven billion people, the ability to find like minds has real value.

Of course, at a time when data privacy is a serious social issue, the question is: who owns the networked future of reading? Publishers might assume they do, but their failure to lead these innovations puts them at risk of becoming redundant. Amazon and the technology giants seem unstoppable. If that's true, we face a future where every book and every comment about it is owned, and profited from, by a handful of major corporations.

Readmill and other developers might yet deliver the future of reading back into the hands of readers and writers. But if this ideal is to become a reality, we're going to have to rethink what it means to own a book, or any kind of information, even if you created it. Perhaps the networked future of reading belongs to no one, and therefore to everyone.

1   In the first paragraph, the writer says he did not understand
    A   why someone had made notes in the book he found.
    B   how his friend could have read such an alarming story.
    C   why someone had left the book on the train.
    D   how the previous reader's notes related to the story.
2   The writer assumes that the reader who wrote the notes
    A   was very critical of the novel.
    B   thoroughly enjoyed the novel.
    C   was a great fan of crime fiction.
    D   was impressed by the writer's informal style.
3   In the writer's opinion, *Readmill* is likely to be particularly successful because it allows readers to
    A   comment on books they are reading.
    B   communicate with other readers.
    C   discuss other readers' comments.
    D   underline passages of text.
4   The additional feature of *Readmill* highlighted in the sixth paragraph allows
    A   a book's author to change what he or she had written.
    B   the writer of a book to join the readers' debate.
    C   readers to ask an author questions.
    D   readers to comment without giving their name.
5   What future development of network reading interests the writer most?
    A   Authors will be able to find out why readers like their books.
    B   Readers will have access to a wide range of book reviews.
    C   Authors will be able to keep in touch with some of their readers.
    D   Readers will be able to contact people with similar ideas.
6   The writer hopes that *Readmill* and similar apps will
    A   make possession of books a more positive experience.
    B   make book publishing more profitable.
    C   strengthen the influence of major publishers.
    D   change how people read and write books.

Part 1

1   Read the text in the Exam task without looking at the four options. Can you think of any words which might fit the gaps?

2   Now do the exam task.

Exam task

For questions **1–8**, read the text below and decided which answers (**A, B, C** or **D**) best fits each gap. There is an example at the beginning.

Example: (0)   **A** defend   **B** protect   **C** argue   **D** preserve

Is classical music still relevant today?

Having listened to this music for more than three decades, I have often had to (0) ___A___ my devotion to classical music against the kind of people who have a very practical (1) _____ to life. I have to admit that I have often been faced with legitimate questions and arguments that made me (2) _____ my ideas. Over the years, I have been lucky enough to live in different (3) _____ of the world. Because of this I have come to the (4) _____ that I belong to a small group of people who believe in artistic principles that have nothing to do with humanity's desire for success or a more comfortable (5) _____ . Quite a few people (6) _____ that this music belongs to the museum and is of (7) _____ only to those who have a particular reason to find out what music was like in the past. In some (8) _____ places I have visited, people simply called it western music and dismissed any possible interest for anybody outside Europe.

1	**A** method	**B** means	**C** way	**D** attitude
2	**A** reorder	**B** rearrange	**C** reorganise	**D** reconsider
3	**A** places	**B** parts	**C** communities	**D** societies
4	**A** conclusion	**B** assumption	**C** decision	**D** deduction
5	**A** presence	**B** lifestyle	**C** being	**D** survival
6	**A** discuss	**B** differ	**C** argue	**D** disagree
7	**A** attention	**B** attraction	**C** influence	**D** interest
8	**A** remote	**B** far	**C** apart	**D** separate

Listening

🎧 **07** You will hear five short extracts in which people talk about their favourite artist.

While you listen you must complete both tasks.

TASK ONE

For questions **1–5**, choose from the list (**A–H**) when each speaker first saw their favourite artist's work.

A later in life
B while on business
C quite recently
D approximately a decade ago
E as a young child
F in their mid-teens
G in the nineteen-fifties
H as a student

Speaker 1	1
Speaker 2	2
Speaker 3	3
Speaker 4	4
Speaker 5	5

TASK TWO

For questions **6–10**, choose from the list (**A–H**) what most impresses each speaker about their favourite artist's work.

A the humour
B the lack of accuracy in the paintings
C the truthful self-portraits
D the countryside paintings
E the classical quality
F the ordinary subject matter
G the sense of mystery
H the technique of applying paint

Speaker 1	6
Speaker 2	7
Speaker 3	8
Speaker 4	9
Speaker 5	10

Grammar

Verbs followed by the infinitive and/or *-ing*

1 Put the verbs in the box into the correct categories in the table below.

> afford ask attempt avoid can catch someone
> continue decide encourage finish force
> forget intend let someone like look forward to
> love make someone may mean might must
> object to offer persuade practise prefer pretend
> promise refuse regret remember remind should
> start stop suggest tell try

infinitive without *to*	can
to infinitive	attempt
someone + *to* infinitive	ask
-ing	avoid
to infinitive or *-ing* (with different meanings)	forget
to infinitive or *-ing* (with similar meanings)	like

2 Choose the correct verb forms *in italics* in these sentences.

1 Have you ever considered *investing / to invest* in art?
2 The man admitted *breaking / to break* into the Louvre.
3 He said he was trying *stealing / to steal* the Mona Lisa.
4 I don't remember *booking / to book* seats for the concert, but I must have done as I have the tickets.
5 I really regret *saying / to say* that I liked Mozart.
6 I wish you'd stop *pretending to know / to pretend knowing* about classical music.
7 Unfortunately, they forgot *renewing / to renew* the insurance on the art gallery.
8 You are not allowed *taking / to take* photos in the museum.

3 Rewrite these sentences using the correct form of the verbs in brackets, like the example.

1 Amy's teacher said she should apply for art college. (*encourage*)
   Amy's teacher encouraged her to apply for art college.
2 Everyone thinks she will be a famous artist. (*expect*)

   ....
3 Amy realises this means working hard. (*involve*)

   ....
4 Tom said he didn't damage the painting. (*deny*)

   ....
5 I can't wait to go to the new musical. (*look forward*)

   ....

Writing

Part 2 Exam task: review

1 Read these extracts from book reviews. Underline any words or phrases which are used to praise the book. Circle those that criticise the book.

1 I found it too heavy and quite difficult to read.
2 I think it is one of the most important and captivating books ever written.
3 I thought it was too wordy which is a real shame, as the story itself is extremely compelling.
4 It's easy to get into and the characters grip you straight away.
5 Perhaps the concept is good but for me it was just too plain and monotonous.
6 The last quarter of the novel just seemed too fantastical and far-fetched to me.
7 This book is truly outstanding, it is a timeless comedy that demands to be read.

2 Write two sentences, the first saying why you liked a particular book, and the second saying why you disliked a different book.

....

....

3 Read this exam task and the model review. Do you think either of these books would interest you?

> You see the announcement below in a magazine aimed at people of your age.
>
> **Classics good and bad**
> Every language has its classic literature, but many young people today don't know which classics are still worth reading. We would like to publish reviews guiding our readers and helping them choose books they would really enjoy reading.
> Send in your reviews of two classics you have read, one you would recommend and the other you would suggest other readers avoid.
>
> Write your **review**.

4 Now write brief answers to these questions.

1 In what ways are the two books similar?
2 How are they different from the reviewer's point of view?
3 Does the model include any useful review phrases that you might be able to use in a review?

> **Two very different books by the same author**
>
> Charles Dickens wrote many books and in this review I am going to contrast two of his novels: one I enjoyed and another that I found hard going.
>
> The book I enjoyed and would thoroughly recommend is *Great Expectations* which combines a thrilling story and a serious consideration of the moral education of Pip, a young boy who is continually cheated but who emerges at the end of the novel as a better person. In my opinion this is an almost perfect novel which traces the relationship between Pip and three other main characters: the criminal Magwitch, the peculiar eccentric Miss Haversham and the beautiful Estella. This is both an exciting and a moving book.
>
> The second work I'd like to consider is *The Pickwick Papers*, a book which I am having to read as part of my English literature degree. I have to admit I am finding it very heavy going and am not sure that I will be able to finish it. For me, Dickens introduces far too many unnecessary characters and this makes the narrative confusing for the reader. Unlike *Great Expectations*, the book has no proper plot for the reader to become involved in and it has a collection of uninteresting characters. Although my tutor finds the book hilarious, the humour does not appeal to me or my fellow students.
>
> To sum up, both these books are written in Dickens' wonderful style, but for today's readers, I would recommend *Great Expectations* for its story and inspiring themes.

5 Now do this exam task. Write your answer in **220–260** words in an appropriate style.

> You see the announcement below in a contemporary magazine aimed at people of your age.
>
> **Contemporary fiction in your language**
> Our readers frequently ask us to recommend works of contemporary fiction from other countries. To satisfy this demand, we are planning to publish reviews suggesting which books our readers might enjoy.
> Send in your reviews of two contemporary works you would recommend to our readers, comparing and contrasting their different features.
>
> Write your **review**.

Reading and Use of English

Part 7 Exam task

You are going to read a newspaper article about clothes and the environment. Six paragraphs have been removed from the article. Choose from the paragraphs **A–G** the one which fits each gap (**1–6**). There is one extra paragraph which you do not need to use.

Is it possible to be green and fashionable?

Despite the huge numbers of people who care about the environment and love clothes, there is a basic contradiction about being green and being fashionable. This is because the fashion industry depends on a constant stream of ever-changing trends, which means you have to keep consuming. However, buying a lot of things that you don't need, in this case new clothes, is harmful to the environment.

1

Firstly, develop your own unique style, so, rather than basing your choice of clothes on whatever the fashion industry says you should, choose your own look. If you do this, you'll look a lot more like an individual, and probably more genuinely stylish. It does not require any sense of style to copy the looks in glossy magazines. It does require some to develop your own. You'll find that because your clothes aren't going in and out of fashion every week, you'll buy fewer and this helps the environment.

2

The problem with buying every changing fashion is that it looks out of date within a few weeks. If you buy a white T-shirt with a slogan because that is the in thing right now, in just a few months, it will look silly. The trend might come round again, but probably not in the same form. On the other hand, if you buy a white T-shirt, it will look fine until it wears out. Opt for simple designs, especially with larger items such as coats.

3

A variation on this is to organise clothes swaps with friends or neighbours. This way, everybody gets new clothes without actually consuming any more resources. You can feel pleased with yourself because you'll have earned a reputation for being green.

4

While we're on the subject of the materials, here is a word of warning. Try to avoid buying clothes made from animal products, especially fur. Not only will this have the effect of reducing animal suffering, it will also reduce your environmental footprint; animal products have a larger impact than plant products because they consume more resources.

5

So, let's imagine you have taken our advice and gone for simple, second-hand, organic clothes, but you still want to enjoy passing trends. The gentlest way to do this is to go for small things like jewellery, bags and shoes which use up fewer resources than an entire new wardrobe every month.

6

In the end, what you wear is your choice and no-one would suggest that this should not be a free choice. But we hope that, having read this, you will be fully aware of the impact your choices may have on the health of our planet.

A If plain-looking clothes don't appeal to you, an alternative eco-friendly option is to buy second-hand clothes. The environmental impact is practically zero as nothing new is being made. If your image of shops which sell second-hand clothes is piles of shabby pullovers and jeans, think again. Find the right shops, and you'll discover a lot of very attractive clothes, often for a lot less than you'd pay for new.

B On the other hand, your clothes habit is probably not the biggest part of your carbon footprint. If being fashionable is important to you, compromise where you can to make the habit a bit greener, and concentrate your planet-saving activities elsewhere. There are a number of simple actions you can take.

C Part of the growing eco-friendly lifestyle includes being mindful not only of what we eat and how we recycle, but also being more aware of what goes into the clothes we buy.

D Remember, too that these are the sort of items widely available from independent producers, meaning that you can support small businesses rather than massive, planet-damaging multinationals. And, if you have any skill with crafts yourself, you could even note the latest trend and make your own version.

E Some people think that another way of achieving this is to buy only natural fabrics, like cotton. But actually the production of some plant-based fabrics involves the use of enormous quantities of pesticides. In fact, cotton is an especially dirty crop, with methods used in its cultivation which can wreck the local environment. If you want to avoid adding to soil and water pollution in this manner, simply opt for organic fabrics.

F This also applies to leather clothing production, which supports the not-very-environmentally-friendly cattle farming industry. However, since leather is a practical material rather than simply a fashion fabric like fur, we'll allow an exception for coats, shoes and boots.

G You can achieve the same effect by buying higher quality clothes because these will not need to be replaced as frequently as a greater number of cheap clothes. This is not only better for the environment, it also means you'll have simpler, more attractive clothes even if they are less obviously stylish.

Part 4 Exam task

For questions **1–6**, complete the second sentence so that it has a similar meaning to the first sentence, using the word given. **Do not change the word given.** You must use between **three** and **six** words, including the word given. Here is an example (0).

Example:

0 It was only after I got home that I realised I'd left my wallet at work.

UNTIL

Not ....UNTIL I GOT HOME............ did I realise I'd left my wallet at work.

---

1 When the management asked for suggestions, several original ideas were made by staff.

CAME

Responding to a management request for suggestions,

....

several original ideas.

2 Lucy was very happy to hear that she'd passed her driving test.

MOON

Lucy ....
heard that she'd passed her driving test.

3 Simon's approach to life is very practical.

EARTH

Simon ....
approach to life.

4 How would you describe his appearance?

LOOKS

Could you tell me .... ?

5 Cities today are not as badly polluted as cities a hundred years ago.

COMPARED

Cities today are .... cities a hundred years ago.

6 The 1970s was the last time fish were seen in this river.

SINCE

Not ....
seen in this river.

Listening

Collocations

Match words from List A with words from List B to make two-word phrases. Write a definition for each phrase.

A   air endangered global habitat renewable solar
B   destruction energy panel pollution species warming

Exam task

🎧 **08**   You will hear three different extracts. For questions **1–6**, choose the answer (**A**, **B** or **C**) which fits best according to what you hear. There are two questions for each extract.

Extract One

You hear two neighbours discussing future energy supplies.

1   They agree that
   A   their region is a good location for wind turbines.
   B   renewable sources of energy should be used.
   C   the appearance of the countryside is important.

2   What does the man have against wind turbines?
   A   He objects to what they look like.
   B   He thinks they are too expensive to build.
   C   He believes they produce insufficient energy.

Extract Two

You hear part of an interview with Carlos Gomez, an architect who designs environmentally-friendly houses.

3   How are Carlos' houses similar to 'normal houses'?
   A   They are built to modern standards.
   B   They are efficient in their use of energy.
   C   They reflect the needs of their occupants.

4   The interviewer assumes the houses designed by Carlos are
   A   outside the price range of most people.
   B   about average in price.
   C   more affordable than ordinary homes.

Extract Three

You hear two managers talking about how their company could reduce the negative impact it has on the environment.

5   What worries the woman about her colleague's suggestion?
   A   She thinks the public may question the company's motives.
   B   She thinks it would not make much difference to the environment.
   C   She thinks it would reduce the company's profits.

6   The woman suggests that the company
   A   uses less plastic packaging.
   B   purchases more food from nearby sources.
   C   reduces the price of the food it sells.

Grammar

Inversion of subject and verb

1   Rewrite these sentences beginning with the words and phrases in brackets.

1   We've hardly ever seen such environmental destruction. (*Seldom*)

2   The storm damaged hundreds of trees and brought down power lines. (*Not only*)

3   You shouldn't smoke if there are young children in the room. (*On no account*)

4   The children weren't in any way to blame for the damage. (*In no way*)

5   It was only in the twentieth century that they started cutting down the rainforests. (*Not until*)

6   People didn't realise that vehicle emissions caused global warming. (*Little*)

7   The ship left the harbour and almost immediately it sank. (*Hardly*)

8   Whatever the situation, fires should not be lit here.   (*Under no circumstances*)

9   I've never seen such a blaze. (*Never before*)

10   You won't see these species anywhere else in the world. (*Nowhere*)

Writing

Part 1 Exam task: essay

Sentence adverbs

1 Rewrite these sentences starting with one of the adverbs in the box. There are two adverbs you do not need to use.

> admittedly   apparently   fortunately   generally
> not surprisingly   obviously   sadly

1 We should save energy whenever we can. That's clear.

....

2 It was very lucky that no one was hurt in the accident.

....

3 Everyone welcomes the tax cuts. That's no surprise.

....

4 There were hardly any butterflies in our garden this summer, which is a real shame.

....

5 This winter will be the coldest on record, so they say.

....

2 Read the exam task and discuss these questions.

1 How might the law and education be used to improve the situation?
2 How do you think the public would react to price rises?
3 Which, if any, of the opinions expressed by panel members do you agree with?

> Your class has attended a panel discussion on what methods governments should use to encourage people to reduce their carbon footprint. You have made the notes below.
>
> **Methods governments could use to encourage people to reduce their carbon footprint**
> - the law
> - price rises
> - education
>
> Some opinions expressed by panel members:
>
> 'People need to be convinced they can make a difference.'
>
> 'All public bodies should set an example.'
>
> 'We should control the use of precious resources like petrol and gas.'
>
> Write an essay for your tutor discussing **two** of the points in your notes. You should **explain which method you think would be more effective, giving reasons** to support your opinion.
> You may, if you wish, make use of the opinions expressed by panel members, but you should use your own words as far as possible.

3 Read the model essay below and answer these questions.

1 Which two notes does the writer refer to and where?
2 Which two opinions does he use and how does he paraphrase them?
3 Which method does he think would be more effective?
4 What reasons does he provide for his choice of method?

Not until recently had anyone used the term "carbon footprint" and yet today it is one of the most common phrases heard when people discuss climate change and global warming. It is generally agreed that the quantity of carbon dioxide resulting from human activity is causing long-term damage to our environment. The question under consideration is this: what can be done to reduce the carbon footprint of businesses and individuals?

One of the solutions put forward to achieve this aim was for governments to bring in new laws to change our use of energy resources. It was suggested, for example, that fossil fuels should be limited in future. Other members agreed that this would be effective, but thought it would be unpopular with the public because it would limit how far they could travel in their cars and their ability to heat their homes.

Another method suggested was that schools should play a leading role in educating future generations about the effect of human behaviour on the environment. It was agreed that the population need to be persuaded more forcefully that individuals should change their behaviour. Many people believe that this process of persuasion should begin in primary schools.

On balance, I would prefer the education route to the use of the law. It is my view that people need to be taught about the problem and to understand how they can contribute to the solution. Laws could have a negative effect if they were felt to be unfair, and this could lead to resentment and lack of cooperation.

4 Now write your own essay in response to this question. Use one different note and one different opinion from those used in the model essay. Write **220–260** words in an appropriate style.

Reading and Use of English

Part 8 Exam task

You are going to read four pieces of advice given to young people looking for employment. For questions **1–10**, choose from the four texts (**A–D**). The texts may be chosen more than once.

Which adviser suggests …

that applicants should show that they are keen on the job they have applied for? **1** ☐

applicants do not pretend to be something they are not? **2** ☐

looking for jobs in less well-known organisations? **3** ☐

applicants should be careful about personal details they make public? **4** ☐

applicants investigate the state of organisations they are applying to? **5** ☐

that how applicants look and sound can make a difference to employers? **6** ☐

that interviews should be two-way conversations? **7** ☐

the kinds of companies applicants should apply to? **8** ☐

ways in which applicants can avoid getting a bad reputation? **9** ☐

there are problems associated with applying for well-advertised jobs? **10** ☐

Adviser A

You should be very conscious of your digital footprint and remember that nothing can ever really be deleted from the Internet. This includes social media profiles such as Facebook, as well as forums and websites. There are three fairly simple ways of cleaning up your online image. Firstly, make sure you control who can see the information you put on Facebook and other sites by using your Privacy settings to allow you to share your footprint only with those you allow as friends. Secondly, you might not be able to fully delete some things from showing up on search engines, but you can use public professional networking sites such as LinkedIn to fill out your profile, skills, interests and qualifications and you will start to build a more professional digital footprint. Finally, getting mentioned for your outside interests can be invaluable, so comment on blogs and articles about things you're interested in or know about. Of course, the only reliable method is to behave well.

Adviser B

If you are applying for a high-profile vacancy, remember that if you've seen it, so have others. If you have had no luck applying for positions this way, look for less obviously visible vacancies. It will be time well spent – because when you find one, there will be less competition than for more widely advertised jobs. Remember that different job-hunting methods work for different organisations. For example, applying blind for junior jobs in the media is unlikely to succeed, but building a network of contacts might. For public-sector jobs, however, networking will not get you an interview – you will have to apply formally like everybody else. If you have only applied to big companies, broaden your search. Try smaller companies who do not advertise so widely. Try to discover how they recruit new employees. Does their website have a "Work for us" page? Try different methods – and remember how successful each method is. Then do more of what works. Your time and energy are limited, so use them wisely.

Adviser C

To prepare for your interview, it's vital that you find out what's happening in the industry as a whole and in the company itself. Find out about any problems or challenges facing the organisation. Think about how to demonstrate this knowledge, either in answering questions or for questions you may ask during the interview. At the interview demonstrate good communication skills; be pleasant to everyone you meet and make good eye contact. Successful candidates demonstrate energy and enthusiasm, so make sure you do this by the way you talk and by your body language. Sound interested and put energy in your voice. You know you will be asked certain questions about your strengths and weaknesses. Prepare answers, but not just the ones you think the interviewer wants to hear, but those based on what you know about yourself and the job. Choose weaknesses that are real but which would not affect your ability to do the job, such as preferring time to make decisions.

Adviser D

I have interviewed plenty of candidates and what I advise is to be yourself. I have never liked candidates who were simply playing the game and telling me what they thought I wanted to hear. What I want to know is who you are, how you might fit into the company, what your contribution could be and whether you can handle the stress. I value truth and confidence in your own ability far more than any game playing. And please, interview me as much as I interview you. As a candidate for a job, don't be too anxious; this is your future, you should be confident enough to show me that you want to get a very good idea of what your potential future will be like and whether the position is something that appeals to you. Be honest, ask questions and don't waste my time. Nothing is worse than wasting the time of a potential employer, who you might meet again one day and will want them to remember you with respect.

For questions **1–8**, read the text below. Use the word given in capitals at the end of some of the lines to form a word that fits in the gap **in the same line**.
There is an example at the beginning (**0**).

Example: (**0**)   COMPULSORY

Education in the USA

It was the state of Massachusetts that first introduced (**0**) .... education in the USA, but by the year 1918, children in every state had to attend school. School starting age, the length of the school year and other (**1**) .... varied depending on the particular state laws governing school (**2**) .... There were two (**3**) .... reasons for the introduction of education for all at this time. The policy was publicised as a (**4**) .... in the common practice of child labour, but in addition to this was a desire by the country's leaders to (**5**) .... the transformation of children into economically (**6**) .... citizens. Since that time, education has (**7**) .... come to be seen as a means of occupying children so as to prevent their involvement in crime and other (**8**) .... activities. To make sure this last aim was achieved, laws were introduced to make the dropping out of school unlawful.

COMPEL

REQUIRE

ATTEND
BASE

REDUCE

SURE
PRODUCE

INCREASE

SOCIETY

Spelling

Fill in the missing words in this table. In each case the missing words have a different internal spelling from the existing words.

Verb	Noun	Adjective
1 give	....	x
2 decide	....	.... (negative)
3	....	clear
4	belief	.... (negative)
5 apply	....	.... (negative)
6	....	long
7 think	....	.... (negative)
8	horror	....

Grammar

Relative clauses

1 Complete these sentences with a relative pronoun. Sometimes more than one answer is possible. If the relative pronoun can be omitted, write –.

1 Make a list of careers .... you think you'd really enjoy, says Mary Phillips, ... works for a company of career consultants.
2 Employers tend to get many open applications .... are not related to any particular jobs.
3 I write informal application letters to employers, ... usually seems to work in my favour.
4 I'd like a job .... challenges me more – something .... demonstrates that I'm a good worker .... simply needs to move on.
5 In any job there will come a time .... you feel you need a new challenge.
6 There is a popular website .... lists the places .... a majority of workers are content.
7 A barber is someone .... job it is to cut men's hair.
8 Could you possibly tell me to .... I should send my application form?

2 ⊙ Here are some sentences written by exam candidates. Two are correct and six are wrong. Tick the correct sentences and correct the wrong ones.

1 Marcia is a 24-year-old student who has just finished a degree in Medicine.

2 Please could you call me at my work number, that you already know?

3 Unfortunately, our office lift is not working, what makes things especially difficult for certain visitors.

4 Greece has many traditions which a few of them look like disappearing in the near future.

5 The work was quite different from what we expected.

6 I worked at a nursery school which I gained experience of dealing with children.

7 I am writing with reference to the article appeared in your newspaper last week.

8 You should avoid working in an environment when speaking your native language is prohibited.

Listening

Part 2

1 Write brief answers to these questions about similarities and differences between English and your language.

1 What are the main grammatical differences?

2 Are there any particular points of grammar you find difficult to understand in English?

3 Are there many words in your language which are similar to English words?

4 How similar or different is your writing system? Do you have a similar alphabet?
How many letters are there in your alphabet?

2 Do the exam task.

Exam task

🎧 **09** You will hear a businessman, Mike Townsend, talking about what he finds difficult about learning a language. For questions 1–8, complete the sentences with a word or a short phrase.

Mike believes that all languages are equally **(1)** .... to learn.

When thinking about language learning, the factor many people forget is the **(2)** .... of the student.

Mike believes people learn a language more effectively if they have a good **(3)** .... to do so.

Knowing some Chinese has helped Mike to do business and to **(4)** .... with people in China.

Mike understands why people are embarrassed by their pronunciation as he himself found certain French sounds **(5)** .... to say correctly.

Mike uses the term **(6)** .... to refer to words that are similar to words in one's language but have a different meaning.

As a learner, Mike's main goal is to learn the **(7)** .... of a language thoroughly.

Compared with learning written Chinese, Mike found Russian **(8)** ....

Writing

Part 2 Exam task: formal letter

Formal language

1 Complete these sentences, which are all from letters of application, with the appropriate word or phrase from the two possibilities given in brackets.

1 I am writing to apply for the job of IT consultant
.... in today's newspaper.
(*as advertised / that you put in*)

2 You will see from my CV that I have
.... to gain extra qualifications.
(*done my best / taken every opportunity*)

3 Please don't hesitate to get in touch if you would like to
....
(*discuss my application further / find out more about me*)

4 I have .... experience from part-time jobs and holiday work.
(*gained valuable / got a lot of useful*)

5 I have spent some time researching your company and have decided I would be interested in
.... of assistant retail manager.
(*applying for the post / going for the job*)

6 I am .... and would welcome the opportunity to join your company on a part-time basis.
(*currently unemployed / out of work at the moment*)

7 .... my application for the post of teaching assistant at your school.
(*I'm enclosing / Please find enclosed*)

8 Thank you for .... my application and I look forward to hearing from you.
(*bothering to read / taking the time to consider*)

2 Read the exam task, think of a company you know and make some notes to answer the task.

> Your company needs to recruit a number of temporary staff to replace employees who are being sent on training courses. Your manager has asked you to write a letter to employment agencies in your city.
> Your letter should explain what the company does, what kind of work temporary staff would do and what qualities the company is looking for in staff.
> Write your **letter**.

3 Read the example answer. The phrases in bold are not appropriate. Write more formal phrases to replace them.

1 .... 4 ....
2 .... 5 ....
3 ....

Dear Sir or Madam,

I am writing to let you know that our company is currently looking for ten employees to replace members of our staff who are about to leave to attend annual training courses next month. We are offering six months' temporary employment **to start with**, but it is possible that the employees we recruit will be offered permanent positions in the future.

Our company has had its headquarters in the city for over fifty years and manufactures a range of building products, including material for insulating buildings. This part of our business has **got much bigger**, as more people look for ways to reduce their energy bills.

We are looking for people to **do different jobs** in our head-office and in our factory. The office jobs are mainly secretarial, but there are also opportunities for experienced personal assistants and people with managerial experience. Factory positions require no prior knowledge or experience but applicants should be physically fit and be **ready to work nights** from time to time.

The qualities we are looking for in people to fill these temporary posts are those we expect from all our employees. Applicants should have experience of working in an office or a factory but **we don't need any special skills**. We expect our employees to be honest, reliable and punctual. Before offering contracts we will contact the references provided by each applicant.

I would be most grateful if you could make suitable applicants aware of the work opportunities we are offering.

Yours faithfully,

Bianca Perez

4 Now write an answer to this exam task in an appropriate style in **220–260** words.

> The university / college you attend is organising a series of open days to show potential future students what it would be like to study at the university / college. Your head of department has asked you to write a letter to schools in your city inviting their students to attend one these days.
> Your letter should explain how these days will be organised, who the open days are intended for, and how the days should be followed up.
> Write your **letter**.

9 Science and technology

Reading and Use of English

Part 5 Exam task

You are going to read a newspaper article about an exciting discovery. For questions **1–6**, choose the answer (**A, B, C** or **D**) which you think fits best according to the text.

Spectacular skull discovery in Georgia

The spectacular fossilised skull of an ancient human ancestor that died nearly two million years ago has forced scientists to rethink the story of early human evolution. Anthropologists, scientists who study human development, unearthed the skull at a site in Dmanisi, in southern Georgia in the west of Asia, where other remains of human ancestors, simple stone tools and long-extinct animals have been dated to 1.8 million years old. Experts believe the skull is one of the most important fossil finds to date, but it has proved as controversial as it is amazing. Analysis of the skull and other remains at Dmanisi suggests that in the past scientists may have been too ready to give different names to species of human ancestors who were discovered at different places in Africa. Many of those names may now have to be wiped from the textbooks.

The latest fossil is the only complete skull ever found of a human ancestor that lived at the time when our predecessors first walked out of Africa. The skull adds to a collection of bones recovered from Dmanisi that belong to five individuals, most likely an elderly male, two other adult males, a young female and a juvenile of unknown sex.

The site was a busy watering hole that human ancestors shared with giant extinct cheetah-like animals, sabre-toothed cats and other beasts. The carcasses of the individuals were found in collapsed dens where carnivores had apparently dragged them to eat. They are thought to have died within a few hundred years of one another. 'Nobody has ever seen such a well-preserved skull from this period,' said Christoph Zollikofer, a professor at Zurich University's Anthropological Institute, who worked on the remains. 'This is the first complete skull of an adult early Homo. They simply did not exist before,' he said. Homo as a species emerged around 2.4m years ago and includes modern humans.

But while the skull itself is spectacular, it is the implications of the discovery that have caused scientists in the field to pause for thought. Over decades excavating sites in Africa, researchers have named half a dozen different species of early human ancestor, but most, if not all, are now on shaky ground. The most recently unearthed individual had a long face, big teeth, and a very small braincase.

The remains at Dmanisi are thought to be early forms of *Homo erectus,* the first of our relatives to have body proportions like a modern human. The species arose in Africa around 1.8m years ago and may have been the first to harness fire and cook food. The Dmanisi fossils show that *Homo erectus* migrated as far as Asia soon after appearing in Africa.

The latest skull discovered in Dmanisi probably belonged to an adult male and was the largest of the collection. It had a long face and big teeth. But at just under 550 cubic centimetres, it also had the smallest braincase of all the individuals found at the site. The odd dimensions of the fossil prompted the team to look at normal skull variation, both in modern humans and chimps, to see how they compared. They found that while the Dmanisi skulls looked different from one another, the variations were no greater than those seen among modern people and among chimps.

The scientists went on to compare the Dmanisi remains with those of supposedly different species of human ancestors that lived in Africa at the time. They concluded that the variation among them was no greater than that seen at Dmanisi. Rather than being separate species, the human ancestors found in Africa from the same period may simply be normal forms of *Homo erectus.*

'Everything that lived at the time of the Dmanisi remains was probably just *Homo erectus*,' said Professor Zollikofer. 'We are not saying that scientists did things wrong in Africa, but they didn't have the reference points we have. Part of the community will like it, but for another part it will be shocking news.'

David Lordkipanidze at the Georgian National Museum, who leads the Dmanisi excavations, said: 'If you found the Dmanisi skulls at isolated sites in Africa, some people would give them different species names. But one population can have all this variation. Five or six names are being used, but they could all be from one family.'

1 The discovery at Dmanisi showed that
  A existing theories of human development were correct.
  B scientists had given our human ancestors the wrong names.
  C previous ideas about human history may have been wrong.
  D some of our human ancestors did not originate in Africa.

2 According to the text, what is special about the most recent find at Dmanisi?
  A It was found in one piece.
  B It belonged to an old man.
  C It was the first human skull.
  D It is African in origin.

3 What had scientists assumed about skulls they had previously found in Africa?
  A They were much older than the skulls found at Dmanisi.
  B They were the remains of several distinct classes of early humans.
  C They belonged to humans who first used fire for cooking.
  D They might have belonged to a type of monkey.

4 How did the skulls found at Dmanisi compare with those of modern humans?
  A They were completely different.
  B They contained smaller braincases.
  C They were much larger.
  D They varied in size to a similar extent.

5 What do scientists now think about early humans found in Africa?
  A They almost certainly belonged to the same species.
  B There were more different species than they had thought.
  C They were of a completely different species from those found at Dmanisi.
  D They were not ancestors of human beings.

6 Who does Professor Zollikofer think will be shocked by the discovery at Dmanisi?
  A people of all kinds
  B everyone involved in archaeology
  C some scientists working in archaeology
  D the people of Dmanisi

Vocabulary

Answer these questions referring to a dictionary if necessary.

1 Does the word *long* in *long-extinct* (line 7) refer to time or shape?
2 *Recovered* (line 20) is a transitive verb meaning to retrieve or salvage. What is the intransitive meaning of this verb?
3 Is a *juvenile* (line 22) young or old?
4 What is the purpose of a *watering hole* (line 24)?
5 What kind of food do *carnivores* (line 27) eat?
6 What is the word *chimps* (line 67) short for?

Part 2 Exam task

For questions **1–8**, read the text below and think of the word that best fits each gap. Use only **one** word in each gap. There is an example at the beginning (0).

Example: (0) WITH

A robot **(0)** .... an artificial brain is learning languages by stringing words and sentences together. Scientists in France have taught the robot to learn speech patterns and even to think before **(1)** .... speaks. Our brains process spoken words in real time and anticipate **(2)** .... is coming next, which allows us to hold meaningful conversations without pausing to stop and think. This is possible **(3)** .... of connections between parts of the brain. Scientists have incorporated an artificial version of this structure into their robot, **(4)** .... is designed to look like a three-year-old human. Their work could help researchers studying the brain by showing which pathways are important in processing language. But **(5)** .... importantly, it could help robots learn more efficiently. **(6)** .... to one of the scientists, 'At present, engineers are simply unable to program all the knowledge required in a robot, but we now know that the way robots acquire their knowledge of the world could **(7)** .... partially achieved through a learning process – in the same way **(8)** .... children.

Listening

Part 3 Exam task

🎧 **10** You will hear an interview in which Karl Mann, a university research scientist, and Laura Fern, a secondary school science teacher, talk about teaching people science. For questions 1–6, choose the answer (**A, B, C or D**) which fits best according to what you hear.

1 Karl Mann starts by talking about his work
   A as a research scientist.
   B with unintelligent people.
   C with non-experts.
   D as a school teacher.

2 Laura Fern assumes that the people Karl works with
   A are not as bright as her students.
   B are over sixty years old.
   C are similar to the people she teaches.
   D are not as young as her students.

3 What does Karl think of the science curriculum Laura describes?
   A He approves of it.
   B He fears it might put students off.
   C He thinks it sounds too theoretical.
   D He thinks it will help students get into university.

4 In Laura's experience as a teacher,
   A girls have a deeper understanding of science.
   B boys and girls perform equally well at science.
   C girls avoid getting jobs which involve science.
   D boys and girls approach science in different ways.

5 Karl points out that the people he works with
   A need to pass tests and exams.
   B have a limited length of time to learn.
   C attend his sessions from choice.
   D are renewing an old interest in science.

6 How does Karl think his approach helps people?
   A It increases their belief in themselves.
   B It helps them manage their daily lives.
   C It enables them to remain healthy.
   D It enables them to understand scientific theory.

Grammar

Modal verbs

1 Complete these sentences using the words in italics and an appropriate modal verb. Sometimes more than one modal verb can be used.

1 Our car broke down on the motorway, so *we / call* a breakdown company.

2 We arrived on time but the meeting was cancelled which means *we / hurry*.

3 I've lost my glasses which means *I / read* my emails this evening.

4 If you feel as ill as you look, *you / go* to work tomorrow.

5 Omar is usually home by now. I suppose *he / get* stuck in a traffic jam.

6 There's no strict uniform policy at this college, so *you / wear* smart clothes if you don't want to.

7 It's important that my application reaches the company tomorrow, so *you / forget* to post my letter.

8 They're expecting us quite early, so if we're going to be late, *we / let* them know.

2 Work out what's happening from these descriptions and make a deduction like the example. Use the following modals in your answers: *must be, can't be, might be*.

1 You haven't seen Ben for some time, but the bathroom door is closed and you can hear water running.
   Ben must be having a shower.

2 There's loud music and people's voices coming from a neighbour's flat.

3 The friend you are with suddenly says "Isn't that your brother?" Your brother is working abroad.

4 You wake in the middle of the night and hear noises coming from your kitchen.

5 Dan has arranged to come to your house at 7 o'clock. At 6.30 there is a knock at your door.

6 You are woken by the sound of your neighbour starting his car. It's earlier than usual.

Writing

Part 2 Exam task: report

Result links

1 Complete these sentences with the correct linking word or phrase from this list. In some cases, more than one answer is possible.

> as a consequence   consequently   in view of
> on account of   or else   otherwise   owing to
> result in

1 Twenty minutes of moderate exercise should
.... slight shortness of breath.
2 The government has accepted that climate change is a fact and has, ... introduced new green policies.
3 The health authority has closed a hospital ward
.... the recent epidemic.
4 Don't forget to check the oil level in your car,
.... you could do serious damage to the engine.
5 .... the high temperatures, many rivers dried up.
6 More snow than usual has fallen this month and
.... transport services have been disrupted.

2 Read the exam task and the model answer which follows. As you read the report, match these headings with the appropriate sections. There are two more headings than you need.

Attracting adults
Conclusion
Environmental concerns
Food and health
Introduction
The importance of science
Useful classes

> Your school or college is thinking of putting on science classes for adults in your neighbourhood. The director has asked you to write a report on the kinds of classes that would be appropriate.
>
> Your report should suggest reasons why such classes are necessary, suggest specific science topics that might be of interest to adults, and suggest ways of encouraging people to attend the classes.
>
> Write your **report**.

Science classes for adults

A ....
Research shows that many adults do not understand basic scientific ideas. In view of the increasing importance of science, it has been suggested that the college puts on science classes for adults. This report focuses on why there might be a need for such classes.

B ....
Today more than ever, scientific ideas are fundamental to everyday life. Many of our daily concerns and interests are related to science. For example, everyone needs to know something about digital technology, to make full use of their computers or mobile phones. Equally important is an understanding of the dangers facing the environment and what can be done to minimise these. Today's adults grew up at a time when these matters were less important. This is why science classes might appeal to adults.

C ....
Most adults I have spoken to freely admit that their knowledge of science is at best out-of-date and at worst non-existent. Consequently, I believe that classes should not assume any prior knowledge or understanding, but should relate to aspects of life that are relevant to the majority of adults. These would include energy use, food science and family health.

D ....
Adults are more likely attend classes they regard as relevant to their lives and needs. Introductory sessions similar to those that would be taught on the course could be organised and the college might also consider sending out a questionnaire to people living in the area asking what aspects of science they would like to know more about.

3 Now do this exam task.

- Remember the word limit is **220–260** words.
- Give readers an indication of what the sections of your report are about.
- Make sure you cover all areas mentioned in the question.
- Don't forget to write your report in an appropriate style.

> Your local council is thinking about organising a science exhibition in the town next summer. You have been asked to write a report on public attitudes to science.
> Your report should describe what the exhibition should be like, say who should be invited to exhibit and suggest ways of publicising the event.
> Write your **report**.

10 A mind of one's own

Reading and Use of English

Part 6 Exam task

You are going to read four reviews of a book about habits. For questions **1–4**, choose from the reviews **A–D**. The reviews may be chosen more than once.

A

This book contains many obvious ideas, but if you are analysing human behaviour, this is almost inevitable. However, it provides a useful framework which enables us to see ourselves more clearly. Rather than choosing to concentrate on peculiar habits, or acting as an all-knowing adviser, the author has assembled a collection of experiments which are relevant to real life. Non-experts should easily grasp the book's central ideas, but rather than reading it from cover to cover, I would suggest picking it up for ten minutes every day because this will enable you to consider everything carefully, and allow you gradually to build up a picture of why you do what you do and give you ideas about how you might change your behaviour. This book will have a greater impact than some others because it focuses on ordinary habits and avoids dealing with more sensational behaviour.

B

I almost didn't get as far as the practical ideas in this book because of basic errors in the introductory comments about the significance of habits. As I was reading, it occurred to me that many of the types of behaviour that the author referred to as habits were not habits in the accepted sense of the word. He also said that habits are not conscious – something that is only partially true. I almost gave up reading, but then the author quoted research on ways in which intentions can be put into practice, and from then on the book improved. He had come across studies which I found interesting and

informative. Unfortunately, insufficient detail on these studies was included, which meant that it was impossible for me to assess their significance. To conclude, I would say that the new research quoted in the chapter on intentions makes up for some of the book's flaws.

C

In addition to wanting more specific examples, I found myself wishing the author had expanded on his practical advice. The book would also have benefited from some interactive material, which I had presumed it would include. An attractive feature of other recent works on similar subjects is the frequent opportunities readers have to test and measure themselves with a variety of simple but highly informative psychological diagnostic tools. Ironically, these weaknesses derive from one of the author's major strengths: namely, his modesty. He does not try to promote his favourite theories or push his own habit cures. Commendably, he allows readers to make their own decisions and implement their own change regimes. For my part, I took away a new found enthusiasm for some long-forgotten techniques and a resolution to avoid sugar in the new year. The book gains by focusing on normal rather than abnormal behaviour.

D

When I bought this book, I imagined it was going to be a sort of guide to giving up bad habits, such as smoking or gambling. I soon realised that it was no such thing, but a very interesting study of human psychology. We are presented with a description of how habits work that is accessible to non-specialists. We find out how and why habits develop, why some habits are necessary – and what can go wrong when our habits get out of control. He considers ways in which we benefit from habits and urges us to work out which habits have a positive influence on our lives and which are negative. It is important to point out that you don't need a degree in psychology to find this book enjoyable. As a non-scientist with a limited knowledge of the subject, I found it well written and easy to follow.

Which reviewer

shares reviewer A's opinion about the main focus of attention in the book?	1
like reviewer C, approached the book, with expectations that were not met?	2
agrees with reviewer D about the kind of readers the book is aimed at?	3
expresses a different view from the others about the writer's definition of the book's subject matter?	4

Part 4 Exam task

For questions **1–6**, complete the second sentence so that it has a similar meaning to the first sentence, using the word given. **Do not change the word given.** You must use between **three** and **six** words, including the word given. Here is an example **(0)**.

Example:

0 Think about your personal strengths when deciding which course to choose.

CONSIDERATION

You should ......TAKE YOUR PERSONAL STRENGTHS INTO.......
......CONSIDERATION...... when deciding which course to choose.

---

1 Ali gets on well with all his colleagues.

TERMS

Ali .... with
all his colleagues.

2 It looks as if Ben's forgotten to let us know that he isn't coming.

SEEMS

Ben .... to
let us know that he isn't coming.

3 I wasn't surprised to find out that Paul had put on weight.

CAME

It .... that
Paul had put on weight.

4 Josh said he'd be in touch as soon as he'd read my email.

BACK

Josh promised ....
me as soon as he'd read my email.

5 I don't want you to tell anyone what I've just said.

RATHER

I .... anyone
what I've just said.

6 I can't wait to go on holiday in the summer.

FORWARD

I .... on
holiday in the summer.

Vocabulary – Three-part phrasal verbs

Complete these sentences with the correct form of the verbs in the box. In each case the two particles which follow the main verb are shown in bold.

check come do face get look
put stand

1 Teachers often tell children that they should
.... **up to** bullies.

2 Some countries have .... **away with** jail
sentences for low-level crime.

3 I believe that politicians should .... **up
to** their responsibilities.

4 Social workers spend a lot of their time
.... **up on** families where children may
be at risk.

5 Tourists who visit our country often ....
up against communication difficulties.

6 Parents of young babies often have to
.... **up with** sleepless nights.

7 Many sports personalities are role models that young
people .... **up to.**

8 Teachers may find it difficult to ....
through to students who have no interest in their
subject.

Grammar

Wishes and regrets

1 Complete these sentences with the correct form of the verbs in brackets.

1 I've always wished I .... an only child.
(*not / be*)

2 If only I .... jobs last year. (*not /
change*)

3 I really wish my parents .... treating me
like a child. (*stop*)

4 I started work when I was 18, but I now wish I
.... to university. (*go*)

5 If only I .... smoking. (*stop*)

6 I wish my friend .... away from our
neighbourhood next year. (*not / move*)

7 I wish I .... taller than I am. (*be*)

8 I wish I .... speak Portuguese. (*can*)

2 Rewrite the following sentences from exercise 1 on page 41 using the verb *regret*.

1 ....
2 ....
4 ....
8 ....

3 Read about some problem situations and write what the people named would say. Use *wish* in your answers. The first one has been done as an example.

1 Amanda didn't spend enough time revising for her exam.
I wish I'd spent more time revising for my exam.

2 Ivan can't find his passport and he needs it tomorrow morning.
....

3 Jorge finds his friend's habit of singing all the time very annoying.
....

4 Martin didn't know his cousin was coming to stay with him.
....

5 Luke is annoyed his brother borrowed his computer without asking.
....

6 Maria eats more chocolate than she should.
....

7 Michelle is a very untidy person.
....

Listening

Vocabulary – Personality adjectives

Complete each sentence with a personality adjective which is opposite in meaning to the words in brackets.

1 She doesn't find talking to people easy. She's very .... (outgoing)

2 I wouldn't leave money around if I were you. Mark is not completely .... I'm afraid. (dishonest)

3 Anna is quite .... – she's spent her whole life in this small village. (sophisticated)

4 Mike loves parties and being with large groups of people. He's very .... (anti-social)

5 It was .... of you to stand up to those bullies. (cowardly)

6 Be careful what you say – Rafa is rather .... at the moment. (insensitive)

7 Despite his success as a sportsman, David is quite .... about his achievements. (arrogant)

8 I always look on the bright side because I'm .... about the future. (pessimistic)

Exam task

🎧 **11** You will hear five short extracts in which people are talking about worries and anxiety.

While you listen you must complete both tasks.

TASK ONE

For questions **1–5**, choose from the list (**A–H**) the signs of worry described by each speaker.

A aches and pains
B a breathing problem
C exhaustion
D forgetfulness
E great fear
F indecision
G persistent cough
H trembling

Speaker 1 [ ] 1
Speaker 2 [ ] 2
Speaker 3 [ ] 3
Speaker 4 [ ] 4
Speaker 5 [ ] 5

TASK TWO

For questions **6–10**, choose from the list (**A–H**) the cause of the worry described by each speaker.

A family matters
B financial affairs
C health fears
D things outside one's control
E the future
F lack of self-confidence
G work related
H world problems

Speaker 1 [ ] 6
Speaker 2 [ ] 7
Speaker 3 [ ] 8
Speaker 4 [ ] 9
Speaker 5 [ ] 10

Writing

Part 1 Exam task: essay

Concession phrases

1 Match the sentence beginnings 1–6 with the endings A–F. Join them with words or phrases from the box. (There are two more than you need.) The first one has been done as an example.

> all the same   even so   maybe   ~~no matter~~   wherever
> whichever   whoever   yet

1 Most children can count on their parents' support
  no matter how badly they behave.
2 The band is so popular that their fans follow them
  ....
3 The weather forecast was dreadful but ....
  ....
4 Max hardly did any revision and ....
  ....
5 You will come into the town from the north ....
  ....
6 Leo earns a lot of money but ....
  ....

A we were determined to go.
B route you decide to take.
C he couldn't afford to buy a house in this part of the city.
D how badly they behave.
E he did very well in the end of term test.
F they're playing.

2 Read the exam task. Which of the three opinions do you agree with?

> Your class has attended a panel discussion on the qualities that make a good leader.
> You have made the notes below.
>
> > **Personal qualities important in a successful leader**
> > • communicates effectively
> > • is persuasive
> > • inspires others
> >
> > > Some opinions expressed in the discussion:
> > > "People recognise leadership when they see it."
> > > "Leaders arise from particular circumstances."
> > > "The key to successful leadership is influence not authority."
>
> Write an essay for your tutor discussing **two** of the qualities in your notes. You should explain **which quality you think is more important** in a successful leader, **giving reasons to support your opinion.**
> You may, if you wish, make use of the opinions expressed in the discussion, but you should use your own words as far as possible.

3 Read this model answer. How many of your ideas does the writer share?

> In all organisations, from clubs to businesses and governments, leaders play an important part in the success or failure of that organisation. Although many people believe that leaders emerge naturally from situations, how effective a leader is depends largely, I believe, on personal qualities. In this essay, I will discuss some of the qualities often associated with leaders, and say which I think is the most important.
>
> It is often said that no leader can be successful, whatever their ideas, if they are unable to communicate effectively with the people in the organisation they are leading. Whether we think of a primary school head teacher or a political leader, the ability to convey ideas to those in the organisation who will have to put them into practice is essential. There are many ways of communicating with others, but in my opinion there is no substitute for face-to-face contact.
>
> This brings me to my second quality: the ability to persuade. Assuming a leader can communicate effectively, he or she must be able to persuade others that he has good ideas. Leaders should not rely on personal charm or their authority; they should be capable of putting over ideas in a way which will convince others that they are right.
>
> To conclude, I believe that successful leaders are those who can influence the people they lead by communicating ideas persuasively and on a personal level. In any kind of democratic organisation, a leader who is not able to do this will be replaced.

Note
The writer of this model has chosen these qualities:
• communicates effectively
• is persuasive.
and has used the second and third opinions.

4 Now write your answer to the same exam task in an appropriate style in **220–260 words** but ...

- include quality 'inspires others'
- make use of the first opinion "People recognise leadership when they see it."

Answer key

Reading and Use of English

Part 7 Exam task

1 D   2 C   3 A   4 G   5 F   6 E   [Para B not needed]

Part 1

1 paparazzi   2 one year   3 Halle Berry's daughter

Exam task

1 D   2 A   3 C   4 A   5 C   6 D   7 A   8 C

Listening

1 1 5   2 dramatic situations   3 3

Part 4 Exam task

1 E   2 H   3 D   4 A   5 C   [Not used: B, F, G]

6 C   7 A   8 F   9 H   10 B   [Not used: D, E, G]

Recording script

You'll hear five short extracts in which people are talking about dramatic situations they have been in.

Look at Task 1. For questions 1–5, choose from the list (A–H) the situation each speaker describes.

Now look at Task 2. For questions 6–10, choose from the list (A–H) how each speaker felt in the situation they describe. While you listen you must complete both tasks.

You now have 45 seconds to look at Part 4.

Speaker 1

I was hurrying to my 6 o'clock yoga class and was already late so I was driving fast. As I approached my turn off, I could see there was quite a tailback. I wondered about going on to the next turning, but by that time I was already committed. In the next fifteen minutes, the queue moved just a few metres and gradually I became aware of a strange smell – like something cooking. An hour later, still crawling along, I could see where the smell was coming from: <u>a burning car on the opposite carriageway</u>. There were ambulances and police cars on the scene. <u>It really shook me up</u> although as far as I could see, there was no one in the car.

Speaker 2

I came out of the college and <u>was astonished</u> to see at least fifteen photographers pointing cameras in my direction. They were shouting things like "Over here" and "Look this way". It took me a moment or two to realise that they were directing their orders at someone behind me, not me.

I looked round and saw the college principal, who was clearly very uncomfortable and was obviously trying to get to his car as quickly as he could. <u>A reporter pushed a microphone in his face</u> and said, "Would you like to respond to the allegations that have been made against you?" The principal looked down and said quietly: "No comment."

Speaker 3

We'd only been away for three days – a weekend break in the country with friends. We'd had a great time – going for walks, doing a bit of cooking, watching our favourite TV programmes and generally relaxing after a hard week at work. It was the Sunday evening when we arrived back. Everything seemed completely normal until we opened the front door – <u>then it hit us</u>. <u>The whole place had been turned upside down – our stuff was all over the floor. It was impossible to see what had been taken</u>, but of course, the first thing we did was call the police. They said we shouldn't move anything – so we just had to sit and wait for them in the middle of our wrecked home.

Speaker 4

I didn't take much notice of the rain to start with, then it got louder and I could hear the wind in the trees but I still wasn't worried. I must have nodded off again because I found myself suddenly awake and <u>deafened by the roaring noise</u>. I looked out of the window just as a huge tree fell down across the road, narrowly missing a car. I phoned the police to warn them to close the road, but just then another tree crashed down, this time hitting a supermarket delivery lorry. <u>I realised how fortunate I'd been</u>. If the wind had been in the opposite direction, I might not be here now.

Speaker 5

I was on holiday having a great time. The last thing on my mind was what was happening at home. My friends and I had spent most of the day on the beach but we decided to pop into a café for a bite to eat before going back to our hotel. The television was on in the café – showing some local soap. The actors were speaking a language we couldn't understand, then suddenly the programme was interrupted by an English voice. <u>Our president had been shot while on an overseas visit</u>, probably by a local terrorist group. The reporter had no idea how serious his injuries were. <u>It was dreadful news but it was not unexpected</u>.

Grammar

1 1 I'd known   2 are currently looking   3 I'll have been studying   4 I was driving; made   5 we arrived; we'd driven   6 I'm going to start   7 I know
8 I've just finished; I'm

2 1 is   2 will have forgotten   3 has been downloading   4 have published; are bringing out   5 had been

3 1 I didn't met → I didn't **meet**

2 we didn't considered → we didn't **consider**

3 were really unsatisfactory → **was** really unsatisfactory; joined → **had** joined

4 I have started → I **started**

5 has being → has **been**

Writing

1 1 Despite **2** In contrast, **3** In spite of the fact that
4 Nevertheless

2 1 two **2** No, only if you wish (but you must use your own words.)

3 1 Nevertheless *or* However **2** Although **3** Despite
4 However

4 Model essay

When an economy is doing badly, it is not unusual for businesses to make older employees redundant. People in their fifties and older are often more seriously affected by unemployment than younger colleagues, because they are less likely to find jobs they are qualified to do with an acceptable level of pay. Frequently, this leads to long-term unemployment among people in this age group. I will now suggest two possible solutions to this problem.

It has been suggested that older unemployed people might share jobs. This arrangement would benefit two unemployed people, but the disadvantage would be that neither would earn the same amount of money as in their previous employment. This, in turn would have a negative impact on their family's standard of living. On the plus side, job-sharing would allow people some free time to pursue other interests, or even to retrain.

This brings me to my second solution to the problem of older unemployed workers: retraining. One of the reasons that it is difficult for this group to find work is that they may not have the skills required by modern organisations. They might be equipped to do basic manual work, but a retraining programme would provide them with skills which would be more attractive to potential employers.

Of these two possible solutions to the problem of long-term unemployment among the over-fifties, I would suggest that retraining would be more likely to help these people back into work because, like everyone else, the over-fifties want to maintain their standard of living and do satisfying work.

Unit 2

Reading and Use of English

Part 6

1 1 The purpose of travel in the 21st century

2 similarities and differences of opinion between the writers

Exam task

1 D 2 C 3 A 4 B

Grammar

1 2 Located in the suburbs, the new mall is very popular.

3 Having been late for college yesterday, he set his alarm for an earlier time this morning.

4 Having completed the project, he started his next venture.

5 Looking over her shoulder, she saw the train leaving.

6 Having taken the wrong train, I found myself in Swindon not Oxford.

7 The man walking the dog is a friend of mine.

8 Not having had / Having not had a break all day, I was desperate for something to eat.

9 Stepping up to the microphone, the presenter cleared his voice.

10 Driven carefully, this car is quite safe.

2 1 Having seen some of the damage done by tourists, I am now a strong believer in eco-tourism.

2 Wanting to boost the economies of the places they visit, eco-tourists try to eat only locally produced food.

3 Having arrived two hours late, the group missed their flight.

4 Being an experienced travel guide, Mario always gives reliable advice about places worth visiting.

5 Having been climbed by large numbers of tourists, Uluru, or Ayers Rock, in Australia is now seriously eroded.

6 Giving Uluru back to the Aboriginal people in 1985, the Australian government hoped that tourists would respect its spiritual significance.

Reading and Use of English

Part 3

1 1 inappropriate **2** deregulate **3** enforce
4 improbable **5** irrational

2 1 recall **2** antisocial **3** interaction **4** outperforming
5 underestimate **6** overexcited **7** biannual
8 misinterpret

3 A New Zealand flag

Exam task

1 accomplishment 2 security 3 cultural
4 incredibly 5 agreeable 6 Surprisingly
7 overcharged 8 peaceful

Listening

Part 2 Exam task

1 fascinated 2 Australia 3 by boat 4 starting point
5 desert 6 underwater camera
7 (personal) highlights 8 glow

Recording script

You will hear a student called Tom Sadler talking about a trip to The Galapagos Islands. For questions 1–8, complete the sentences with a word or short phrase.

You now have 45 seconds to look at Part 2.

You always hear that the Galapagos Islands are a once-in-a-lifetime opportunity to see lots of unusual wildlife both on land and in the sea, as well as unspoilt natural landscapes. After spending a week there, I can tell you that these islands are definitely something special. They are incredibly beautiful, totally unique, and filled with such a diversity of life. (1) You can see why Darwin was so fascinated by them.

Before I went there myself, (2) I didn't even really know where the islands were – I thought somewhere between Australia and Indonesia, but actually they're in the Pacific a thousand kilometres off the west coast of South America – more or less on the Equator. They're not that hard to get to by plane from Ecuador – amazingly, there are actually two flights a day. (3) You can get there by boat but it's at least a three-day voyage. I suppose it would have been quite interesting to arrive in the same way as Darwin did, but sadly I didn't have the time.

4) I arrived at the starting point on Santa Cruz where my trip started out by trying to coax the famous giant tortoises out of hiding, so that I and the others in the group could take photos of them. Unfortunately, they were nowhere to be found. They'd probably had enough of strangers flashing lights in their faces. It was a bit disappointing, but luckily we found some later on in the day and took photos of them instead.

Our days on the islands were pretty much the same. In the morning, we would set off on a hike before it got too hot. We would go looking for birds, reptiles, and different types of plants. (5) I was constantly amazed by the diversity of the landscape here. It often went from desert to jungle on the same island. Most afternoons, we would go diving. This was my favourite part of the tour. The islands themselves were great but what's below the surface of the water is where the Galapagos are really spectacular.

There's much more life below the water than above it. What I saw has only been rivalled by what I saw when I went diving on the Great Barrier Reef. (6) I'm still kicking myself for not taking an underwater camera with me.

My whole trip was wonderful and (7) I could give you a minute-by-minute description. I won't do that, but here are just a few of my personal highlights. Firstly swimming with sea creatures. One of the sea turtles we swam with actually swam into me – thank goodness it didn't do me any damage. On another occasion, a sea lion chased me for a few minutes. I have to admit I was rather worried to start with but he didn't attack me – I think he was just curious. On the same day, I spotted an octopus that was hiding in some rocks – it was difficult to see because it looked exactly the same as the rocks it was hiding in.

Then, on our last night, (8) dolphins swam with the boat and seemed to glow in the dark. They even did some flips – a perfect ending to a perfect trip.

Writing

Part 2

1 1 **To sum up**, what we must do is encourage the next generation to do sports.

2 It also includes **recommendations / a recommendation** for improvements to help the department operate efficiently.

3 Despite the problems I **have outlined**, I enjoyed attending this conference.

4 **In short,** everything's organised for you.

5 In order to **consider** appointing someone as my assistant, you have asked me to write this report outlining my needs

6 The purpose of this report is **to suggest** the most suitable catering company.

7 **Having considered all the above**, I believe that my proposal meets your requirements.

8 I'd like **to suggest some** improvements to the week's programme.

2 1 A tourist region in your country.

2 For a tutor. To look at the impact of tourism.

3 The place and its popularity; the impact on the region; changes that would improve the region.

3 **1** Yes **2** Yes **3** Government action to reverse the damage ; Businesses should be encouraged to be more environmentally friendly.

4 The historical background: *It was known to the ancient Mayan tribes*

The effect on the original town: *With regard to the impact tourism has had*

The reason for its popularity: *Tourists are attracted to Cancun for many reasons*

Specific examples of the impact: *A nearby rainforest has shrunk in size*

Unit 3

Reading and Use of English

Part 5 Exam task

1 B **2** D **3** B **4** D **5** C **6** A

Part 4

key word	Which part/s of the first sentence must you replace
0 profile = noun	attempted not to attract attention
1 attention = noun	ignored
2 turning = verb	wishes she had accepted the (job) offer
3 talked = verb	persuade her not to resign
4 keep = verb	continue / high level
5 meeting = verb	why don't we get together
6 point = noun	you won't achieve anything if you refuse

Exam task

1 pay attention to   **2** regrets turning down the offer
3 talked out of resigning   **4** keep up the high level
5 suggested meeting (up)   **6** no point (in) refusing

Listening

Part 1

Extract one: Two friends talking about an article they read.
Extract two: Two students discussing a presentation they have to give.
Extract three: Two friends talking about living alone.

Exam task

1 C **2** C **3** A **4** A **5** B **6** C

Recording script

You will hear three different extracts. For questions 1–6, choose the answer (A, B or C) which fits best according to what you hear. There are two questions for each extract.

Extract One

You hear two friends discussing an article they have both read.

Now look at questions one and two.

Female: Have you seen this article?

Male: Fascinating, wasn't it? I loved the fact that it was a scientific and psychological analysis.

Female: Yes, actually (1) it looks at what goes on in the brain during childhood instead of just complaining about teenagers' behaviour.

Male: Yes, or why teenagers are much worse today than they used to be. I thought that part was fascinating.

Female: Oh, and the idea that teenagers aren't irresponsible, but just overestimate the rewards.

Male: Yes, apparently they're more motivated by rewards than any other generation and because of this, they take more risks. It was also interesting that we become better decision-makers as we get older.

Female: That's just common sense, isn't it? The more experience you have, the better decisions you can make – hardly a revolutionary idea.

Male: I know, but the way they linked it to the development of part of the brain made it more interesting.

Female: True, but what really stood out for me was the idea that people remain directionless into their twenties or thirties. (2) Learning so many different subjects and topics is making kids more intelligent, but delaying the development of part of their brain.

Male: Yes, and that's the part that makes them highly skilled or expert at something.

Female: I can really relate to that. I spent years wondering what I should do.

Extract Two

You hear two students discussing a group presentation they have to give.

Now look at questions three and four.

Tom:	So have you finished your part of the presentation yet?
Hannah:	Nearly, I just need to finish off the bibliography. How about you?
Tom:	I'm all done. I really just need to practise now. (3) <u>Do you think Nick will turn up today?</u>
Hannah:	I've no idea. Your guess is as good as mine.
Tom:	Doesn't it bother you?
Hannah:	Of course, but what can we do about it?
Tom:	He's hardly ever here. I doubt he's made much progress with his part. This presentation is worth thirty per cent of the module, so we have to do something about it. I think we need to speak to the tutor.
Hannah:	I can't see that working. (4) <u>He'll just say that's one of the challenges of teamwork and expect us to sort it out.</u>
Tom:	<u>You're right.</u> Let's get in touch with Nick again.
Hannah:	We could, but it probably won't get us anywhere. I think we should just write his bit as well and plan to do it without him.
Tom:	Really? What if he turns up on the day?
Hannah:	Well, we'll give him the notes and tell him what to say. Either way we're covered and we'll know it's done, so we won't have to stress.
Tom:	Good point. Let's do it.

Extract Three

You hear two friends talking about living alone.

Now look at questions five and six.

Claire:	How's the new flat?
Anthony:	I love it, but it's a bit quiet. (5) <u>I haven't got used to the lack of atmosphere with no other flatmates.</u>
Claire:	<u>For me that's probably the only downside.</u> Think about all the pluses – shower when you want it, not tidying up after other people, watching what you want on TV.
Anthony:	True, but I do miss the social side, you know, someone to chat to in the evening – apart from colleagues at work, I can spend days not seeing someone else.
Claire:	Yes, but now you don't get people pinching your food from the fridge.
Anthony:	(6) <u>I was probably one of the worst for stealing food!</u> So would you ever live with someone again?
Claire:	I don't know. If I had to for financial reasons I probably would, but unless I really had to I wouldn't.
Anthony:	You used to love living in our house.
Claire:	I did, but that was years ago. It's fantastic when you're in your twenties, but you get to a point in your life when you want your own space.
Anthony:	So never again?
Claire:	Why, do you need a flatmate?
Anthony:	No, no, just curious.
Claire:	Perhaps when I'm old and can't get out of the house.

Grammar

1　**1**　verb + *that*: accept, admit, agree, argue, complain, deny, explain, suggest

　　2　verb + object + *that*: advise, convince, inform, persuade, promise, remind, tell, warn

　　3　verb + *to* infinitive: agree, promise

　　4　verb + object + *to* + infinitive: persuade, remind, tell, warn

　　5　verb + *ing*: deny, suggest

2　**1**　Rita agreed (that) she could really relate to that.

　　2　Hannah explained (that) she just needed to finish off the bibliography.

　　3　Hannah thought (that) he would just say it was one of the challenges of teamwork.

　　4　Tom suggested getting in touch with Nick again. / Tom suggested that they get in touch with Nick again. / Tom suggested they (should) get in touch with Nick again.

　　5　Anthony admitted (that) he hadn't got used to the lack of atmosphere with no other flatmates.

　　6　Anthony complained (that) he could spend days not seeing someone else.

　　7　Anthony reminded Claire (that) she used to love living in their house.

3　**1**　Ben asked Hannah what she thought the weather was going to be like the following day.

　　2　Scott wanted to know if / whether Peter could lend him some money until the following week.

　　3　John asked Ed if / whether he had watched the match the previous night / the night before.

　　4　Tom wondered if / whether anyone had seen his phone.

　　5　Maria asked Juan what time he would be home that night.

Writing

1 **1** people **2** so can't **3** take part / go in for **4** As well as this / On top of that **5** so much information / such a lot of information **6** Let's meet / Shall we meet

2 **1** To find out in more detail what has been happening to "you" at work.

    2 In what ways the boss treats "you" differently / worse than other employees.

    3 Help

3 **1** paragraph 2 **2** paragraph 1 **3** paragraph 3 **4** paragraph 5 **5** paragraph 4

4 **1** I'm sorry **2** got me down **3** Basically **4** row **5** are supposed to **6** a word **7** putting me down **8** tells me off **9** workmates **10** I dread **11** feeling **12** make things better

5 **Model answer**

> Dear Penny,
>
> Thanks for your letter – it's really good to hear from you, and thanks for asking about my studies.
>
> You suggest that I may be wondering whether the subjects I've opted to take are the right ones. When I chose these subjects about this time last year, I was really interested in history and thought it was something I was pretty good at. Unfortunately, my last history exam results were disappointing and, as a result, I've lost a bit of confidence and some of the interest I had in history. The other subjects, economics and politics are fine – I'm really enjoying them. I can drop history at the end of this year, but I've got to pass an end of year test and revising for that is what's difficult at the moment. I think when you've decided to drop a subject, remaining interested is quite difficult.
>
> As for your suggestion that I may have more interesting things on my mind, you're absolutely right. The main thing is that I've finally got a social life. The last two years have been really hard work for me, but now I'm relaxing a bit and I'm spending quite a lot of time hanging out with my friends. Of course, this makes studying more difficult. So it's not that I've lost interest in my studies as a whole, but just that I've found new ways of spending some of my time.
>
> Anyway, that sums up my situation. How are things with you? Hope to hear from you soon.
>
> Best wishes

Unit 4

Reading and Use of English

Part 7 Exam task

    1 E **2** D **3** G **4** A **5** C **6** F [Para B is not needed]

Part 2 Exam task

    1 as **2** comparison **3** however **4** would **5** to **6** made **7** had **8** result

Vocabulary

    1 unaffordable; incomes; make ends meet **2** gross; overdrawn **3** interest; taxed **4** overheads **5** loss; break even; profit

Grammar

1 **1** <u>It has been proved</u> that shoplifting …

    2 <u>It will be claimed</u> that teenagers …

    3 <u>It is said</u> that credit cards are …

    4 <u>It is thought</u> that the money …

    5 <u>It has been shown that</u> teenagers …

2 **1** People's spending habits **are influenced** by different factors.

    2 As you probably know, **a good level of English is needed** in order to attend that university. *Or* As you probably know, you need a good level of English in order to attend that university.

    3 This custom **has been disappearing** lately.

    4 England **(has) qualified** for the finals of the World Cup.

    5 The story **is set** in the 30s.

Listening

Part 3 Exam task

1 B   2 D   3 C   4 A   5 A   6 B

Recording script

You will hear an interview in which two journalists, Jonathan Wood and Laura Key, are discussing the subject of foreign aid to poor countries. For questions 1–6, choose the answer (A, B, C or D) which fits best according to what you hear.

You now have 70 seconds to look at Part 3.

Interviewer:	I think most of us would agree, wouldn't we, that the gap between rich and poor countries is one of the most difficult problems of the modern age? And what can be done to help poor countries to move out of poverty has been the subject of fierce debate for many years now. Sadly, this problem hasn't gone away and the solutions are no clearer now than they were fifty years ago. So what are your thoughts on this? Jonathan, can I start with you?
Jonathan:	Sure. Like most people, I used to think that if large amounts of money were given to the governments of underdeveloped countries, the situation in those countries would gradually improve. Unfortunately, this has not always been the case, for a variety of reasons. And I'd say this has made some people in the donor countries rather cynical – especially when there is relative poverty in their own countries. So, (1) although most people are willing to give to charities working in poor countries, they are less supportive of their own governments handing over millions of pounds or dollars which could be used at home.
Interviewer:	Laura, do you agree? Are the public in developed countries becoming less generous?
Laura:	I wouldn't say they're becoming less generous, perhaps just a bit more cautious about who money is given to and (2) most importantly, how it is spent. Most of us are willing to give to help people who are ill or starving, but we want to be sure that our money reaches the people who need it and doesn't get used to fund the luxury lifestyles of politicians or officials.
Jonathan:	That's it exactly, but I would add that in recent years, organisations which give practical assistance rather than just money seem to be doing a better job of helping people and countries out of poverty than large donations of cash from government to government.
Interviewer:	What kinds of assistance are you thinking of?
Jonathan:	You know, building schools or hospitals, (3) sending doctors and nurses armed with life-saving drugs, providing teachers – these are all good examples.
Laura:	I agree, Jonathan – there are also some fantastic projects which help people to improve their farming practices so that they can produce more food. We've recognised for a long time that it's better to help people to produce their own food than simply to give them food hand-outs. And, of course, (3) connected to this, trying to improve health services.
Interviewer:	But you'd agree, wouldn't you, that there are times when food hand-outs are essential?
Jonathan:	Of course. It's obvious that in famine situations where large numbers of people are at risk, we have to provide immediate food aid. But we should always remember that this is only a short-term measure and (4) we need to have longer-term strategies which help people to provide for themselves.
Laura:	Yes, and it would be the same if a population was threatened by an epidemic of some kind. The international community and particularly the richer countries would be duty bound to provide medical treatment to save lives, but then there are health issues which are ongoing, but where aid is needed for projects which require initial funding. A good example of this would be making sure communities had permanent, reliable sources of clean water.
Interviewer:	Then there's the subject of aid money which poor countries are obliged to spend on goods and services from the donor countries. Is that something you have views about?

Laura:	It certainly is. I think this is basically a dishonest practice, aimed partly at boosting the economies of the donor countries rather than helping poor countries to become successful and independent. I would say that this is one of the objections some people have to giving large sums of money to foreign governments. The people who benefit from this kind of aid are often the wealthier sections of the populations of the poor countries. The money is sometimes even used to buy guns and tanks to be used in regional conflicts. This is undoubtedly wrong (5) <u>but above all, the poor won't benefit at all</u>.
Jonathan:	I don't entirely agree with that, Laura. (6) <u>As long as the receiving government is not corrupt</u>, then tied aid like this can be beneficial to both countries, people in the poor countries are helped and thousands of people in wealthy countries have secure employment.
Interviewer:	But that does depend on openness and honesty on both sides, doesn't it?
Jonathan:	Of course, that goes without saying.

Writing

1 **1** children's health; demands on parents
    2 Children's health: obesity more of a problem
      Demands on parents: children's influence on family spending
    3 Opinion 1: also about the growing influence children have over household spending. Advertising can lead to parents feeling obliged to give in to their children's unreasonable demands.

2 **1** for example **2** to **3** however **4** Firstly **5** but
    6 in fact **7** Not only **8** Such **9** own view
    10 In the end

6 Model answer

Economists have shown that unless people save money regularly, they will have a lower standard of living after they retire than during their working life. Everyone used to save for their retirement pension, but today many people prefer to live for the present rather than thinking about the future. Experts now say that the savings habit should start when people are young. In this essay, I will consider ways of persuading young people to save.

It has been suggested that parents and other adults should make sure children are aware of what their future likely needs will be and then insist that they save a small proportion of their allowance or their income. This need only be 5%, but it would establish the principle of regular saving.

Youngsters might object that they need all their money for daily living now and that they cannot afford to save. The answer to this objection would be that young people should reduce their current spending by a small amount and then save what they don't spend. This might mean buying fewer snacks or drinks, or spending less on their mobile phone.

To conclude, I recommend that young people reduce their current spending and save what they don't spend, taking account of their likely future needs. If everyone does this, young people will soon get used to the idea of saving regularly. They could check their accounts occasionally to assure themselves that their savings are increasing in value. Hopefully, in this way they will realise that their life will be more comfortable in the future.

Unit 5

Reading and Use of English

Part 8

1 Suggested key words and phrases

1 be put off; previous experience
2 expected; be worse than it was
3 training programme; go more quickly
4 previous injury; prevent them from competing
5 avoid walking; physical problem
6 without weighing up the advantages and disadvantages
7 wanted to complete a race
8 celebrating an important event
9 good physical condition prior
10 motivated; watching the end of a marathon

Exam task

1 B 2 A 3 E 4 D 5 E 6 B 7 C 8 D 9 A 10 C

Part 3

1

Noun	Verb	Adjective	Adverb
activity	hospitalise	attractive	certainly
archaeologist	lengthen	awful	mentally
decision	modernise	comfortable	obviously
friendship	modify	dangerous	
frustration	qualify	friendly	
kindness	sharpen	healthy	
mentor		hopeless	
nutrition		medical	
participant		therapeutic	

2 1 verb → adjective 2 adjective → adjective
3 noun → adjective 4 adjective → verb 5 verb → adjective
6 verb → adjective 7 noun → adjective 8 noun → negative noun

Exam task

1 responsible 2 deadly 3 remarkable 4 weaken
5 harmless 6 effective 7 optimistic 8 discomfort(s)

Listening

Part 2

1 1 prevention 2 clinical 3 surgery 4 consciousness
5 medical

Exam task

1 fascinating 2 sweating 3 change his lifestyle 4 (great) relief 5 progressive 6 natural 7 (too) energetic
8 determined

Recording script

You will hear Phil Matthews, a medical student, giving a presentation to fellow students about a member of his family with diabetes. For questions 1–8, complete the sentences with a word or short phrase.

You now have 45 seconds to look at Part 2.

Hi, everyone. As you'll remember, we've been studying diabetes recently. (1) I've found our lectures particularly fascinating because my father has just found out he has the disease, so I've been able to see how it affects someone's life. As we all know, there are two kinds of diabetes: Types 1 and 2. There is nothing that can be done to prevent type 1 which often occurs in early life, but, apparently there are steps that can be taken to avoid type 2, such as regular exercise and a healthy diet. My dad's in his late fifties, did hardly any exercise and didn't have a particularly healthy diet. He'd been feeling slightly unwell for some time, often experiencing (2) the symptoms of low blood sugar: dizziness, sweating and weakness. He went to his doctor on several occasions and each time (3) he was told to change his lifestyle. On one occasion he was sent to the gym to encourage him to take more exercise. The doctor should have told him he was at risk of developing diabetes. I think if he had, my dad would have taken his condition more seriously.

Anyway, six months ago, he went for a routine blood test and the result showed that he was diabetic. (4) I remember he was pretty shocked when he found out, but he also felt relief because it explained why he had been feeling unwell. Although there have been trials showing that with extreme diet control, the symptoms of diabetes can be reversed, my dad was told that the condition cannot be cured. They said he might be able to stop it getting worse by losing weight, exercising regularly and controlling his diet. As we've found out from our studies, some people manage to control the illness for years, but (5) it is a progressive condition and most patients eventually need to take medication to control their blood sugar. I've used my dad as a case study for a project I'm doing. As I'd expect of him, (6) he tried the natural way for a few months, but it didn't work and after a year, he was prescribed tablets. He has to attend a special diabetic clinic every three months, where they test his blood, weigh him, and check his eyesight. Diabetes causes nerve damage and this can affect various parts of the body, for example your heart and your eyes, so all diabetics have to have these regular check-ups. He says he feels okay most of the time, (7) but he gets tired if he does anything too energetic. He doesn't complain much, but I think underneath, he's actually quite worried. (8) Watching my dad cope with diabetes has made me determined not to make the mistakes he made, but he hasn't let it ruin his life and I admire him for that.

Grammar

1 **1** hadn't taken   **2** phone   **3** I'd / would ask
4 wouldn't be   **5** is   **6** he'd / would be playing

2 **1** If you don't stick to your calorie-controlled diet, you won't lose weight.
2 Only if I felt really ill, would I go to the doctor.(*Notice inversion because of **only***)
3 I'd have lost my tooth if I hadn't gone to the dentist yesterday afternoon.
4 Provided you take regular exercise, you'll stay fit and healthy.
5 He would have been ill more frequently if he hadn't kept to a healthy diet.

Writing

1 **1** to / in order to / so as to help   **2** due to   **3** so that / so   **4** in order to / so as to / to   **5** because   **6** so as not to   **7** to / in order to / so as to   **8** because of

4 **(Suggested answers)**

1 aim: purpose; object   **2** suggest: recommend; propose
3 This means: Consequently; Because of this; The consequence of this is   **4** frequently: often; regularly
5 benefit: gain   **6** as: since; because   **7** For this reason: Because of this; With this in mind; Therefore; That's why
8 currently: now   **9** not uncommon: common; normal; not unusual   **10** problems: difficulties   **11** At the moment: Currently

5 **Model answer**

> Introduction
> The aim of this proposal is to suggest ways in which traffic accidents in our town can be prevented or reduced.
> Reduced speed limits
> It has been shown that many serious accidents and almost all those resulting in deaths and serious injuries are caused by drivers going too fast. In view of this, it has been suggested that the speed limits in the town's residential are reduced from the current limit of 50 kph to 30 kph. Clearly this would not prevent accidents entirely, but would result in fewer deaths and injuries.
> Traffic calming measures
> In addition to the introduction of reduced speed limits, it has been suggested that traffic calming measures are introduced. Such measures, which have proved very effective in other places, would force people to drive more carefully to avoid damaging their vehicles. Examples of traffic calming measures include the building of speed bumps across roads, the so called "sleeping policemen", as well as more mini-roundabouts at small crossroads.
> Safety barriers
> Currently, many of the roads coming into our town from surrounding areas have one or two lanes in each direction but have no safety barriers between the two sides. This has resulted in a number of very serious crashes. The construction of a central barrier to separate cars going in opposite directions would eliminate accidents of this kind.
> Conclusion
> I believe that any of the above measures would reduce accidents. However, I would strongly recommend that all three measures are introduced as soon as is practical.

Reading and Use of English

Part 5 Exam task

1 C   2 A   3 C   4 B   5 D   6 A

Part 1 Exam task

1 D   2 D   3 B   4 A   5 B   6 C   7 D   8 A

Listening

Part 4 Exam task

2 1 E   2 H   3 A   4 C   5 F   (B, D and G not used)
   6 H   7 B   8 C   4 A   10 F   (D, E and G not used)

Recording script

Part 4 consists of two tasks. You'll hear five short extracts in which people talk about favourite artist. Look at Task 1. For questions 1–5, choose from the list (A–H) when each speaker first saw their favourite artist's work.

Now look at Task 2. For questions 6–10, choose from the list (A–H) what most impresses each speaker about their favourite artist's work.

While you listen, you must complete both tasks.

You now have 45 seconds to look at Part 4.

Speaker 1

People often ask me why I love Vincent van Gogh's paintings. I don't suppose my reasons are very different from other people's - they just leave me open-mouthed. I clearly remember the first time I saw an exhibition of his work about fifteen years ago, the bright colours and wild shapes made me so dizzy that I had to sit down. His brushstrokes seemed to be flying off the canvas and coming towards me. Many years before that, when I was about eight or nine, I remember staring at *Starry Night* - probably his most famous painting after *Sunflowers*. It wasn't the painting itself - just a picture in a book belonging to my dad. I remember thinking how much I'd like to have been out on that night looking up at the stars.

Speaker 2

I can trace my obsession with Picasso's work back to a visit to Paris as <u>part of my degree course</u>. I love Picasso for one of the things he is most criticised for: the fact that he didn't paint well. I've had many arguments with people who don't consider his paintings good because they can't recognise instantly the things he paints. But they miss the point. I say that he 'didn't' paint well, not that he 'couldn't' paint well. His early works show that he had incredible skill, but he threw it all away because he wasn't interested in painting what you could see with your eyes, <u>he was interested in painting what you couldn't see but what was equally real</u>.

Speaker 3

I only became aware of Rembrandt <u>in my early fifties</u> but I think he's an extraordinary artist. I particularly like the paintings he did of himself – if you look at them in the order in which they were painted, you can see how <u>he documented with great honesty</u> and in detail his progress from being a carefree young man through to being a frail old man. As we reach old age, most of us prefer not to see ourselves as we really are, and go about our daily lives without thinking too much about our changing lives. Remarkably, by contrast, Rembrandt doesn't shy away from the subject – he keeps on looking even though he almost certainly fears and dislikes what he sees.

Speaker 4

It wasn't until I'd seen Magritte's work in a London exhibition <u>a few months ago</u>, that I realised just how funny his stuff was. People walk around these exhibitions with a serious expression – <u>I just walked round laughing uncontrollably</u>. Until then, I'd always thought of Magritte as having an interesting and intriguing mind, but suddenly here he was, this wonderfully dry joke teller. The work that really struck me was *The Man in the Bowler Hat*. He'd spent months painting the man and then he painted a bird flying in front of the man's face. What's happened there could happen only in a photograph and he'd done a painting of it. I thought he was so clever.

Speaker 5

I first came across David Hockney when my father took me to an exhibition of his work in a small gallery in London. <u>I must have been about 15</u>, I suppose. Dad was an amateur painter himself and he'd read about Hockney but never seen any of his paintings. Unfortunately he was disappointed by what he saw, but I was completely fascinated – particularly by the themes of his paintings. <u>They were sort of everyday events</u> – people in domestic situations – not the themes of great classical paintings like battles, rural landscapes or important people. And his use of colour really hit me. I remember one painting: *A Bigger Splash* – it's quite famous now. The colours are simple and bright. It has a very clean look.

Grammar

1   **infinitive without *to*:** can, let someone, make someone, may, might, must, should

   to **infinitive:** afford, attempt, decide, intend, mean, offer, pretend, promise, refuse

   someone + *to* **infinitive:** ask, encourage, force, persuade, remind, tell

   ***-ing*:** avoid, catch someone, finish, look forward to, object to, practise, suggest

   to **infinitive or *-ing* (with different meanings):** forget, regret, remember, stop, try

   to **infinitive or *-ing* (with similar meanings):** continue, like, love, prefer, start,

2 1 investing   **2** breaking   **3** to steal   **4** booking   **5** saying
    6 pretending to know   **7** to renew   **8** to take

3 **2**   Everyone expects her to be a famous artist.
    3   Amy realises this involves working hard.
    4   Tom denied damaging the painting.
    5   I'm looking forward to going to the new musical.

Writing

1 **1**   I found it too heavy and quite difficult to read.
    2   I think it is one of the most important and captivating books ever written.
    3   I thought it was too wordy which is a real shame, as the story itself is extremely compelling.
    4   It's easy to get into and the characters grip you straight away.
    5   Perhaps the concept is good but for me it was just too plain and monotonous.
    6   The last quarter of the novel just seemed too fantastical and far–fetched to me.
    7   This book is truly outstanding, it is a timeless comedy that demands to be read.

4 **(Suggested answers)**
    1   Same author; wonderful style
    2   Great Expectations – strong plot; The Pickwick Papers – weak plot; Great Expectations – interesting characters; The Pickwick Papers – unnecessary characters
    3   Praising phrases: (a book I) would thoroughly recommend; a thrilling story; an almost perfect novel; written in (Dickens') wonderful style
       Criticising phrases: I am finding it very heavy going; this makes the narrative confusing; no proper plot; humour does not appeal to me

Unit 7

Reading and Use of English

Part 7 Exam task

1 B   **2** G   **3** A   **4** E   **5** F   **6** D   [Para C not needed]

Part 4 Exam task

    1   (the) staff came up with
    2   was over the moon when she
    3   has a very down to earth
    4   what he looks like
    5   not as badly polluted compared with / to
    6   since the 1970s have fish been

Listening

Part 1

    air pollution – harmful chemicals in the atmosphere
    endangered species – type of animal at risk of becoming extinct
    global warming – increase in temperature of the world's atmosphere
    habitat destruction – serious damage to areas where animals live
    renewable energy – power sources which cannot be used up
    solar panel – a device that changes energy from the sun into electricity

Exam task

    1 B   **2** C   **3** C   **4** A   **5** A   **6** B

Recording script

You will hear three different extracts. For questions 1–6, choose the answer (A, B or C) which fits best according to what you hear. There are two questions for each extract.

Extract 1

You hear two neighbours discussing future energy supplies.

Now look at questions one and two.

Woman: I don't understand what the problem is. As I see it, we need to make more use of renewable energy and I imagine wind turbines are one of the obvious ways of doing this. I thought most people agreed on that.

Man: Well, I agree with the first part of what you said, but not the second. We definitely do need to use renewable alternatives as much as we possibly can, I just don't think wind turbines are the best way of doing this?

Woman: But this part of the country's the perfect place, isn't it? I mean we're quite high up and the wind blows most of the time up here. You're not one of those people who think they spoil the look of the countryside, are you? I think that's a really short-sighted attitude.

Man: No, actually – I quite like their appearance.

Woman: Oh, really?

Man: Yes, in fact I'd say they're quite attractive.

Woman: So what's the problem, then?

Man: I have two issues with them; the first is that making each turbine consumes a huge amount of energy and in the end they don't actually produce very much power.

Extract 2

You hear part of an interview with Carlos Gomez, an architect who designs environmentally-friendly houses.

Now look at questions three and four.

Woman: So, tell me Carlos, you advertise yourself as a 'green architect' – how exactly are you different from a normal architect?

Carlos: Well, a lot of what I do is exactly the same as what a normal architect does. So, for me, the appearance and comfort of my houses are essential. The design of every house I build is based on what the people who are going to live in the house want. Their requirements and tastes come first for me, but in addition, my buildings have to be eco-friendly.

Woman: Okay, but what does that mean in practice?

Carlos: Well, all my buildings have triple-glazed windows and roofs made of solar panels. This means that they require almost no heating. But in addition, rainwater is collected and recycled, so minimising the use of externally supplied water. And all waste products are processed and can be used as compost in the garden.

Woman: That's very impressive, but I guess your houses cost a fortune – more than ordinary home-buyers could afford.

Carlos: Of course the initial construction costs are comparatively high, but you have to remember that the running costs of my houses are very low compared with those of traditional buildings.

Extract 3

You hear two managers talking about how their company could reduce the negative impact it has on the environment.

Now look at questions five and six.

Woman: So we have this meeting in two weeks' time and we've got to come up with some suggestions. Have you had any thoughts?

Man: I've had a few initial ideas, and I'd suggest we do something to reduce the amount of packaging we use in our stores. That would help to reduce our costs and be a benefit to the environment. And we could publicise this in a new advertising campaign to prove what a responsible business we are. We might even attract new customers.

Woman: Not a bad idea Ben, but we'd have to make sure people didn't think we were doing it just to increase our profits.

Man: Of course, but I'd see that as a win-win situation. We spend less on plastic wrappings and boxes, and our customers have less to carry home and throw away.

Woman: I don't disagree with that, but what about trying to buy more of the food we sell locally – that would mean our lorries didn't have to travel so far, which in turn would also reduce our costs, and benefit local farmers.

Man: And it would reduce air pollution caused by our vehicle emissions.

Woman: Good thinking – a great idea, Ben.

Grammar

1 **Seldom** have we seen such environmental destruction.
2 **Not only** did the storm damage hundreds of trees, it also brought down power lines.
3 **On no account** should you smoke if there are young children in the room.
4 **In no way** were the children to blame for the damage.
5 **Not until** the twentieth century did they start cutting down the rainforests.
6 **Little** did people realise that vehicle emissions caused global warming.
7 **Hardly** had the ship left the harbour when it sank.
8 **Under no circumstances** should fires be lit here.
9 **Never before** have I seen such a blaze.
10 **Nowhere** else in the world will you see these species.

Writing

1 1 Obviously, we should save energy whenever we can.
  2 Fortunately, no one was hurt in the accident.
  3 Not surprisingly, everyone welcomes the tax cuts.
  4 Sadly, there were hardly any butterflies in our garden this summer.
  5 Apparently, this winter will be the coldest on record.

3 1 the law – Paragraph 2; education – Paragraph 3
  2 Two opinions used:
  • We should control the use of precious resources like petrol and gas.
  • People need to be convinced they can make a difference.
  Paraphrase: *the population need to be persuaded more forcefully that individuals should change their behaviour*
  Paraphrase: *fossil fuels should be limited in future.*
  3 Education
  4 People need to be taught about the problem and to understand how they can contribute to the solution rather than be subjected to new laws which they might see as unfair.

Reading and Use of English

Part 8 Exam task

1 C   2 D   3 B   4 A   5 C   6 C   7 D   8 B   9 A   10 B

Part 3 Exam task

1 requirements   2 attendance   3 basic   4 reduction
5 ensure   6 productive   7 increasingly   8 antisocial

Spelling

	verb	noun	adjective
1	give	gift	
2	decide	decision	decisive / indecisive
3	clarify	clarity	clear
	(also *clear*)		
4	believe	belief	believable / unbelievable
5	apply	application	applicable / inapplicable
		applicant	
6	lengthen	length	long
7	think	thought	thoughtful / thoughtless
			(also *unthinkable*)
8	horrify	horror	horrific

Grammar

1   1 which / that / – ; who   2 which / that   3 which   4 which /
that; which / that; who / that   5 when   6 which / that; where
7 whose   8 whom

2   Sentences 1 and 5 are correct
   2 my work number, **which** you already know?
   3 our office lift is not working, **which** makes things
   4 many traditions' **a few of which** look like
   6 nursery school **where** I gained
   7 the article **which / that** appeared in your
   8 in an environment **where** speaking

Listening

Part 2 Exam task

1 difficult   2 motivation   3 reason   4 socialise
5 (really) tricky   6 false friends   7 spoken form   8 (quite)
straightforward

Recording script

You will hear a businessman, Mike Townsend, talking about what he finds difficult about learning a language. For questions 1–8, complete the sentences with a word or a short phrase.

You now have 45 seconds to look at Part 2.

With my trip to Brazil coming up later in the year, I'm doing a crash course in Portuguese, and I've been thinking about what makes learning a language difficult. You often hear people say: "Oh, Japanese, that's really hard" or "Isn't Arabic supposed to be impossible to learn?" I did French at school and found that very difficult but since then I've had to learn other languages and found them much easier. In the end (1) <u>I don't think that any language is actually any more difficult to learn than any other</u>. Essentially, the degree of difficulty depends on differences between a learner's own language and the language they're learning. (2) <u>And then what is frequently forgotten when considering this subject is the learner's motivation</u>.

Looking back, I think French was difficult for me because (3) <u>I had no reason to learn it</u> – it was just another school subject, whereas since then I've had real reasons to learn languages. For example, I learnt basic Chinese so that I could do business in China. It was important for me to show people that I had taken the trouble to learn some of their language. As well as helping me to understand and talk technical issues and money matters, (4) <u>knowing some Chinese means that I can also socialise with people I meet</u>. I learnt Spanish at university so I'm hoping I won't find Portuguese too difficult – they're similar languages.

One of the biggest problems for English learners, of course is the idea of gender. When I was learning French, I never understood why tables were feminine – someone told me that in German they're masculine, but now I realise of course that tables themselves aren't masculine or feminine – it's the words that have a gender. And of course pronunciation can be a problem. British people feel embarrassed if they make pronunciation mistakes. I can understand that. (5) <u>Going back to French, I found the pronunciation of the letter "r" really tricky</u>. And I know that the French find the English "th" sound a real problem.

Then there's the problem of vocabulary. (6) Languages often have words that look and sound similar to words in your language but have completely different meanings – so-called false friends. I remember at school I always made the mistake of thinking the French word "librairie" meant library in English, but it doesn't – it means bookshop. And apparently in Portuguese "educado", which looks like "educated" actually means polite. So that can be a cause of problems and difficulties, too.

I know when I'm learning a language, (7) my primary aim is to master the spoken form, because I want to be able to communicate with people I meet on my travels. In lots of languages, the written form is quite different from the language people speak and of course not all languages have the same alphabet or scripts. Having to learn a whole new script, such as Arabic, must cause real problems. From this point of view (8) I found Russian quite straightforward, but Chinese very difficult.

Writing

1 1 as advertised   **2** taken every opportunity   **3** discuss my application further   **4** gained valuable   **5** applying for the post   **6** currently unemployed   **7** Please find enclosed   **8** taking the time to consider

3 Suggested answers

Phrases		Suggested replacements
1	to start with	in the first instance
2	got much bigger	grown considerably
3	do different jobs	fill a variety of positions
4	ready to work nights	prepared to work night shifts
5	we don't need any special skills	no specific skills are required

4 Model letter

Dear Sir or Madam,

I am writing on behalf of the university to let you know that we are in the process of organising a series of open days to show prospective students what studying with us would be like. We would be grateful if you could draw this opportunity to the attention of your final year students.

The open days will take place during the first week of November and be organised by the different departments of the university. Students interested in finding out about Geography, Physics or Engineering should attend on Monday. Our Language, Literature and History departments will be open on Tuesday, and the Creative Arts department, including Music, Art and Drama can be visited on Wednesday. On these days visitors will be able to talk to staff and students currently studying in these departments.

Thursday and Friday of the same week will be general information days when students can find out about applying for courses, accommodation and other such matters. There will also be a number of talks from senior university staff on these days.

As I have indicated in my opening paragraph, our days are intended primarily for students in their final year at secondary school and intending to apply for university, but younger students may also visit if they wish.

Following their visits students may wish to arrange individual meetings with departmental staff or to put in applications for one of our courses.

We look forward to welcoming your students to one of our open days.

Yours faithfully,

Unit 9

Reading and Use of English

Part 5 Exam task

1 C   2 A   3 B   4 D   5 A   6 C

Vocabulary

1 time   It means having been extinct for a long time
2 to get better after an illness
3 young   *juvenile* can be used as a noun or an adjective
4 a pool where animals go to drink
5 meat
6 chimpanzees

Part 2 Exam task

1 it   2 what   3 because   4 which   5 more / most
6 According   7 be   8 as

Listening

Part 3 Exam task

1 C   2 D   3 A   4 B   5 C   6 A

Recording script

You will hear an interview in which Karl Mann, a university research scientist, and Laura Fern, a secondary school science teacher, talk about teaching people science. For questions 1–6, choose the answer (A, B, C or D) which fits best according to what you hear.

You now have 70 seconds to look at Part 3.

Interviewer: We have two guests in the studio today, Karl Mann, a university research scientist and Laura Fern, a secondary school science teacher. Karl, I believe you spend part of your spare time (1) introducing science to people who know little or nothing about the subject. Tell us a little about that.

Karl: Well, I believe that there are many people today who found science difficult when they were at school and this has had two effects: it closes their minds to the wonders of science and it makes them feel stupid. My aim is to introduce them to a few relatively simple ideas.

Interviewer: Laura, as a teacher, would you agree with what Karl says about school science?

Laura: Yes, to an extent, but I believe that in recent years, teachers have made science accessible to a wider range of students than was the case in the past. (2) I think Karl is probably referring to older people, people who were at school in the sixties and seventies.

Interviewer: Is Laura right, Karl? Do the people you work with tend to be older?

Karl: Yes, in general, but I meet a few people in their twenties who also seem to have a mental block as far as science is concerned.

Interviewer: Could you describe how teaching has changed in recent years, Laura?

Laura: Well, firstly, we've made the subject less theoretical. In practice this means we do more laboratory experiments. And secondly, as far as possible, the topics we focus on relate to the real world. So, for example in Biology, we study the effect drugs can have on the body, and in Physics we compare ways of heating buildings efficiently.

Interviewer: Karl, how do you react when you hear that teachers are putting less emphasis on theory?

Karl: (3) I'm all for it. The important thing is that we show students how science is relevant to their everyday lives. Above all, we want to avoid putting them off the subject. If they find practical science interesting, there is no reason why they shouldn't study more theoretical ideas later, for example by choosing to study science at university.

Interviewer: Have you noticed any connection between gender and scientific understanding? I mean traditionally, science was seen as a boys' subject. Is that still the case?

Karl: I think that's still true, yes.

Laura: (4) Sorry, but in my experience, there is generally almost no difference between boys and girls. In fact, in some of the classes I've taught recently, one or two girls have shown more understanding and insight than boys.

Karl:	That's very good news. We need more girls to take up careers in science.
Interviewer:	How do you account for this shift, Laura?
Laura:	I'm not sure. I'd say it's partly due to the curriculum changes I mentioned earlier, but there may also be a social explanation. In the past, girls were not encouraged to consider careers in science. They are now encouraged to regard themselves as the equals of boys in all areas – and I think that's a major reason why more girls are studying science at university level.
Interviewer:	Can we go back to your work, Karl? What exactly do you do with your groups? I mean, how do you awaken their interest in something they've already rejected?
Karl:	The first thing I'd say is that my approach takes time, there's no quick fix. But importantly, unlike in Laura's situation, (5) <u>nobody forces my students to come to my classes</u>.
Laura:	So, they are motivated?
Karl:	Exactly. That's the best possible start. Secondly, there are no tests or exams for my students to fail – that removes some of the fear and makes them more open to new ideas. Then, my curriculum consists of practical case studies which look at the scientific ideas behind familiar everyday issues. For example, my first case study is called "Travelling to work". This introduces different fuels used by various forms of transport and looks at the damaging effect the resulting pollution can have on the environment and on people's health. Another topic is "Healthy eating", a subject close to everyone's heart. We analyse different foods and look at the effects they have on our bodies. They find these topics interesting, but also (6) <u>I believe they develop confidence</u> which will allow them to go on to study more theoretical topics.
Laura:	This sounds very similar to the new school science curriculum I work with, but of course my students have to take tests and exams!

Grammar

1 **1** we had to call a breakdown company
   2 we needn't have hurried
   3 I won't be able to / can't
   4 you shouldn't / mustn't go to work
   5 he might have got stuck
   6 you needn't / don't have to wear smart clothes
   7 you mustn't forget

8 we should let them know

2 (Suggested answers)
   2 The neighbours must be having a party.
   3 It can't be my brother. He's working abroad.
   4 Someone might be cooking a meal. / Someone might be stealing my belongings.
   5 It might be Dan. / Dan might be knocking at the door.
   6 My neighbour must be going to work early this morning.

Writing

1 **1** result in   **2** consequently; as a consequence
   3 on account of; owing to: in view of   **4** otherwise; or else   **5** owing to; on account of   **6** as a consequence; consequently

2 **A** Introduction   **B** The importance of science
   C Useful classes   **D** Attracting adults

3 Model answer

> **Science for all**
>
> As you may know, our council is planning a science fair in the town next year. The purpose of this report is to investigate public attitudes to science and make suggestions about the nature of this fair.
>
> **Public attitudes**
>
> From a survey of friends and acquaintances of all ages, I have drawn the following conclusion: the vast majority of people are interested in many different science subjects. Significantly, however, over half these people say they were put off science at school and still find scientific ideas difficult to grasp. This situation worries them, so a science fair would be welcome if it took a different approach from that taken by their teachers.
>
> **Components of a science fair**
>
> The kind of fair suggested by people would consist of a series of basic talks by experts from different scientific fields. For example, an agriculturalist might be invited to talk about increasing crop production, while a computer scientist might explain how search engines find the information people need. In addition to this, companies could be asked to participate in an exhibition which shows the importance of science to their business. For example, a food company might be asked to show how they produce low-fat products.
>
> **Publicity**
>
> To proceed with the plan, the council must be convinced that people will attend. Television advertising as well as posters need to be ready well in advance of the date of the fair, but perhaps more importantly all forms of publicity should show clearly what aspects of science will be highlighted by the fair.

Reading and Use of English

Part 6 Exam task

1 C   2 D   3 A   4 B

Part 4 Exam task

1 is on good terms   2 seems to have forgotten   3 came as no surprise to me   4 to get back to   5 would/'d rather you did not / didn't tell   6 'm / am looking forward to going

Vocabulary

1 stand   2 done   3 face   4 checking   5 come
6 put   7 look   8 get

Grammar

1 1 was not / wasn't / were not / weren't   2 hadn't / had not changed   3 would stop   4 had gone   5 could stop
6 wasn't / was not moving   7 were / was   8 could

2 1 I've always regretted being an only child.
   2 I regret changing jobs / having changed jobs last year.
   4 I regret not going to university.
   8 I regret not being able to speak Portuguese.

3 **Suggested answers**
   2 I wish I could find my passport. I need it tomorrow morning.
   3 I wish you wouldn't sing all the time.
   4 I wish you'd let me know you were coming to stay.
   5 I wish you'd asked before you borrowed my computer.
   6 I wish I could stop eating chocolate. / I wish I didn't eat so much chocolate.
   7 I wish I wasn't / weren't (such) an untidy person. / I wish I wasn't / weren't so untidy. / I wish I was / were less untidy. / I wish I was / were a tidier person.

Listening

1 shy   2 trustworthy / honest   3 naïve   4 sociable
5 courageous / brave   6 sensitive   7 modest
8 optimistic

Part 4 Exam task

1 H   2 E   3 C   4 F   5 B   [Not needed: A,D,G]
6 G   7 B   8 D   9 E   10 C   [Not needed: A, F, H]

Recording script

You'll hear five short extracts in which people are talking about worries and anxiety. Look at Task 1. For questions 1–5, choose from the list (A–H) the signs of worry described by each speaker.
Now look at Task 2. For questions 6–10, choose from the list (A–H) the cause of the worry described by each speaker.
While you listen you must complete both tasks.

You now have 45 seconds to look at Part 4.

Speaker 1

When I was younger, I worried all the time, about anything and everything. In my mid-twenties especially, I had what I can only describe as extreme anxiety – mostly to do with my job. I'd wake up in the middle of the night shaking – and the worst of it was that it was never a single worry. It was about lots of different things. One worry would lead to another, so, for example, I might start thinking about the wording of an email I'd sent to my manager and end up thinking I might lose my job – and there'd be lots of other related worries in between. Looking back at that time now, all the worries seem very trivial.

Speaker 2

The thing I worry about more than anything else is money – and if I'm not careful I can become helpless with terror at the thought of running out of it. But instead of thinking of a practical solution to the problem, like ways of making more or spending less – I just worry and because I'm not thinking straight, the problem doesn't go away – you know, even if I'm busy doing something, it's there at the back of my mind. Then suddenly, the answer will come to me and the worry disappears. Of course, some of the problems are not real at all – they're just imaginary. They're the worst kind in some ways.

Speaker 3

Experience has shown me that there is a definite link between my being very tired and being worried. It seems that if I'm worrying about something it makes me weary. Night is always the worst time. I often lie awake for hours worrying before I manage to get to sleep – then in the morning, whatever the worry was doesn't seem so bad. As I've got older, I've realised that something that seems really serious at the time means nothing after a few months or years. People tell me I worry most about situations or problems I'm powerless to do anything about – they're probably right. And I always imagine the worst that can happen.

Speaker 4

I was permanently stressed and always worrying about <u>what lay ahead</u>. This made me <u>unable to make up my mind</u> about things in case I made mistakes. My whole life was chaotic and I just couldn't figure out how to deal with all the uncertainty. I had a family that depended on me and I had rent and other things to pay. All the stress affected my life at home, my personal relationships and it made me ill. Eventually I realised that I was in a spiral of anxiety, constantly worrying about the unknown. But over the last few years, I've started feeling better - I think because I've understood how to accept the chaos and live with it.

Speaker 5

For as long as I've known Julie, she's been in an almost permanent state of anxiety. Even when she was very young, she <u>worried about being ill.</u> So, for instance, she was sure she was going to get a mystery illness which doctors wouldn't recognise. She worried so much that she lost her appetite. Then, in her early teenage years, she started having panic attacks at night – <u>she'd wake up out of breath</u>. This was treated successfully and for a few years everything was fine, then when she left home to go to college, the attacks started again. She's now taking tablets but still feels nervous and tense for much of the time.

Writing

1   **2**   wherever they're playing.
    3   all the same / even so we were determined to go.
    4   yet he did very well in the end of term test.
    5   whichever route you decide to take.
    6   even so / yet / all the same he couldn't afford to buy a house in this part of the city.

Notes

Acknowledgements

Development of this publication has made use of the Cambridge English Corpus (CEC). The CEC is a computer database of contemporary spoken and written English, which currently stands at over one billion words. It includes British English, American English and other varieties of English. It also includes the Cambridge Learner Corpus, developed in collaboration with Cambridge English Language Assessment. Cambridge University Press has built up the CEC to provide evidence about language use that helps to produce better language teaching materials.

This product is informed by the English Vocabulary Profile, built as part of English Profile, a collaborative programme designed to enhance the learning, teaching and assessment of English worldwide. Its main funding partners are Cambridge University Press and Cambridge English Language Assessment and its aim is to create a 'profile' for English linked to the Common European Framework of Reference for Languages (CEF). English Profile outcomes, such as the English Vocabulary Profile, will provide detailed information about the language that learners can be expected to demonstrate at each CEF level, offering a clear benchmark for learners' proficiency. For more information, please visit www.englishprofile.org

The authors and publishers acknowledge the following sources of copyright material and are grateful for the permissions granted. While every effort has been made, it has not always been possible to identify the sources of all the material used, or to trace all copyright holders. If any omissions are brought to our notice, we will be happy to include the appropriate acknowledgements on reprinting.

The publisher has used its best endeavours to ensure that the URLs for external websites referred to in this book are correct and active at the time of going to press. However, the publisher has no responsibility for the websites and can make no guarantee that a site will remain live or that the content is or will remain appropriate.

Text

p. 4 adapted from 'The rise of citizen journalism' (Burke, J) 03/10/2006, World Association of Newspapers and News Publishers with permission; p. 5 adapted from 'New law to protect children from paparazzi' 26/09/2013, Sky News with permission; p. 8 adapted from 'The Purpose of Travel' (Basho), Basho – outsidecontext.com with permission; p. 10 adapted from 'Kirsty's Travel Blog: My first solo trip', World Nomads.com; p .12 adapted from 'The impact of social media on children, adolescents and families' (Schurgin O'Keeffe, G and Clarke-Pearson, K), reproduced with permission from PEDIATRICS Vol. 127 No. 4 April 1, 2011 pp. 800–804 Copyright 2011 by The American Academy of Pediatrics (AAP); p. 16 adapted from: 'Money weakens ability to savour life's little pleasures' (Yong, E), 25/05/2010, *Discover Magazine*, with permission from Ed Yong; p. 20 (Text A), adapted from 'My first marathon' NHS Choices; p. 20 (Texts B, C, D, E), adapted from 'First Marathons' (Funderburke, D, Coelho, J, ShewThengChang; Bass, W)

www.marathonguide.com; p. 24 adapted from 'Who owns the networked future of reading?' (Mc Cafferty, H), 23/08/2013, The Guardian © Guardian News & Media Ltd 2013; p. 25, adapted from 'Why and how important is Classical music in our modern way of life' with permission from the Gramophone forum; p. 26 adapted from 'Why I love Picasso' (McCafferty, H) 20/09/2012, *Swide Magazine*, www.swide.com with permission; p. 26 adapted from 'René Magritte: enigmatic master of the impossible dream' (Carter, I) 19/06/2011, *The Guardian*, © Guardian News & Media Ltd 2011; p. 28 adapted from 'Seven quick ways to green fashion' 19/08/2012, CarbonOn.Me; p. 28 from 'How eco-friendly is your clothing' (Phelps, P) 28/08/2013, with permission from Paula Phelps; p. 32 adapted from 'Graduate jobs advice from the experts' (Response 28 to article), 17/07/2011, *The Guardian*, © Guardian News & Media Ltd 2011; p. 36 'Skull of Homo erectus throws story of human evolution into disarray' 17/10/2013, The Guardian, © Guardian News & Media Ltd 2013; p. 37 from 'Watch this childlike humanoid robot begin to comprehend language,' by Rebecca Boyle, copyright 2013. Reprinted with permission; p. 40 (Text C), 'Making Habits, Breaking Habits: Why We Do Things, Why We Don't, and How to Make Any Change Stick' with kind permission from Psych Central.

Photos

Thanks to the following for permission to reproduce copyright photographs:

p. 4 Christopher/Alamy; p. 5 Pictorial Press Ltd/Alamy; p. 6 Rosemary Roberts/Alamy; p. 9 Stanislav Fosenbauer/Shutterstock.com; p. 10 Hemis /Alamy; p. 11 EPA European Pressphoto Agency b.v./Alamy; p. 12 Makenboluo/Shutterstock.com; p. 16 Monkey Business Images/Shutterstock.com; p. 18 Garo/Phanie/ SuperStock; p. 19 Stock Connection/SuperStock; p. 20 Patrick Ward/Alamy; p. 24 Racorn/Shutterstock; p. 25 Ferenc Szelepcsenyi/Shutterstock; p. 26 Peter Horree/Alamy; p. 28 Caro/Alamy; p. 30 Petr Kopka/Shutterstock; p. 33 Time & Life Pictures/Getty Images; p. 34 Moodboard/Alamy; p. 36 AFP/Getty Images; p. 37 AllOver images/Alamy; p. 38 Vladgrin/Shutterstock.com.

Picture research and text permissions: Sarah Deakin

Illustrations: Mark Duffin: pp. 15, 40; Nick Duffy: pp. 22, 42

Recordings by Leon Chambers at The Soundhouse Ltd

Editor: Judith Greet

Project Manager: Jane Coates